THE GOSPEL ACCORDING TO LUKE

AUTHORIZED (KING JAMES) VERSION

Trinitarian Bible Society

Tyndale House, Dorset Road, London, SW19 3NN, England

THE GOSPEL ACCORDING TO

ST. LUKE

1 Forasmuch as many have taken in hand to set forth in order a declaration of those things which are most surely believed among us, ²even as they delivered them unto us, which from the beginning were eyewitnesses, and ministers of the word; ³it seemed good to me also, having had perfect understanding of all things from the very first, to write unto thee in order, most excellent Theophilus, ⁴that thou mightest know the certainty of those things, wherein thou hast been instructed.

The birth of John the Baptist foretold

⁵There was in the days of Herod, the king of Judaea, a certain priest named Zacharias, of the course of Abia: and his wife *was* of the daughters of Aaron, and her name *was* Elisabeth. ⁶And they were both righteous before God, walking in all the commandments and ordinances of the Lord blameless. ⁷And they had no child, because that Elisabeth was barren, and they both were *now* well stricken in years.

⁸And it came to pass, that while he executed the priest's office before God in the order of his course, ⁹according to the custom of the priest's office, his lot was to burn incense when he went into the temple of the Lord. ¹⁰And the whole multitude of the people were praying without at the time of incense.

¹¹And there appeared unto him an angel of the Lord standing on the right side of the altar of incense. ¹²And when Zacharias saw *him*, he was troubled, and fear fell upon him. ¹³But the angel said unto him, Fear not, Zacharias: for thy prayer is heard; and thy wife Elisabeth shall bear thee a son, and thou shalt call his name John. ¹⁴And thou shalt have joy and gladness; and many shall rejoice at his birth. ¹⁵For he shall be great in the sight of the Lord, and shall drink neither wine nor

strong drink; and he shall be filled with the Holy Ghost, even from his mother's womb. 16And many of the children of Israel shall he turn to the Lord their God. 17And he shall go before him in the spirit and power of Elias, to turn the hearts of the fathers to the children, and the disobedient to the wisdom of the just; to make ready a people prepared for the Lord. 18And Zacharias said unto the angel, Whereby shall I know this? for I am an old man, and my wife well stricken in years. 19And the angel answering said unto him, I am Gabriel, that stand in the presence of God; and am sent to speak unto thee, and to shew thee these glad tidings. 20And, behold, thou shalt be dumb, and not able to speak, until the day that these things shall be performed, because thou believest not my words, which shall be fulfilled in their season.

21And the people waited for Zacharias, and marvelled that he tarried so long in the temple. 22And when he came out, he could not speak unto them: and they perceived that he had seen a vision in the temple: for he beckoned unto them, and remained speechless.

23And it came to pass, that, as soon as the days of his ministration were accomplished, he departed to his own house. 24And after those days his wife Elisabeth conceived, and hid herself five months, saying, 25Thus hath the Lord dealt with *me* in the days wherein he looked on me, to take away my reproach among men.

The annunciation to Mary

26And in the sixth month the angel Gabriel was sent from God unto a city of Galilee, named Nazareth, 27to a virgin espoused to a man whose name was Joseph, of the house of David; and the virgin's name *was* Mary. 28And the angel came in unto her, and said, Hail, *thou that art* highly favoured, the Lord *is* with thee: blessed *art* thou among women.

29And when she saw *him*, she was troubled at his saying, and cast in her mind what manner of salutation this should be. 30And the angel said unto her, Fear not, Mary: for thou hast found favour with God. 31And, behold, thou shalt conceive in thy womb, and bring forth a son, and shalt call his name JESUS. 32He shall be great, and shall be called the Son of the Highest: and the Lord God shall give unto him the throne of his father David: ³³and he shall reign over the house of Jacob for ever; and of his kingdom there shall be no end. ³⁴Then said Mary unto the angel, How shall this be, seeing I know not a man? ³⁵And the angel answered and said unto her, The Holy Ghost shall come upon thee, and the power of the Highest shall overshadow thee: therefore also that holy thing which shall be born of thee shall be called the Son of God. ³⁶And, behold, thy cousin Elisabeth, she hath also conceived a son in her old age: and this is the sixth month with her, who was called barren. ³⁷For with God nothing shall be impossible. ³⁸And Mary said, Behold the handmaid of the Lord; be it unto me according to thy word. And the angel departed from her.

³⁹And Mary arose in those days, and went into the hill country with haste, into a city of Juda; ⁴⁰and entered into the house of Zacharias, and saluted Elisabeth. ⁴¹And it came to pass, that, when Elisabeth heard the salutation of Mary, the babe leaped in her womb; and Elisabeth was filled with the Holy Ghost: ⁴²and she spake out with a loud voice, and said, Blessed *art* thou among women, and blessed *is* the fruit of thy womb. ⁴³And whence *is* this to me, that the mother of my Lord should come to me? ⁴⁴For, lo, as soon as the voice of thy salutation sounded in mine ears, the babe leaped in my womb for joy. ⁴⁵And blessed *is* she that believed: for there shall be a performance of those things which were told her from the Lord.

⁴⁶And Mary said, My soul doth magnify the Lord, ⁴⁷and my spirit hath rejoiced in God my Saviour. ⁴⁸For he hath regarded the low estate of his handmaiden: for, behold, from henceforth all generations shall call me blessed. ⁴⁹For he that is mighty hath done to me great things; and holy *is* his name. ⁵⁰And his mercy *is* on them that fear him from generation to generation. ⁵¹He hath shewed strength with his arm; he hath scattered the proud in the imagination of their hearts. ⁵²He hath put down the mighty from *their* seats, and exalted them of low degree. ⁵³He hath filled the hungry with good things; and the rich he hath sent empty away. ⁵⁴He hath holpen his servant Israel, in remembrance of *his* mercy; ⁵⁵as he spake to our fathers, to Abraham, and to his seed for ever.

⁵⁶And Mary abode with her about three months, and returned to her own house.

The birth of John the Baptist

[57] Now Elisabeth's full time came that she should be delivered; and she brought forth a son. [58] And her neighbours and her cousins heard how the Lord had shewed great mercy upon her; and they rejoiced with her. [59] And it came to pass, that on the eighth day they came to circumcise the child; and they called him Zacharias, after the name of his father. [60] And his mother answered and said, Not *so*; but he shall be called John. [61] And they said unto her, There is none of thy kindred that is called by this name. [62] And they made signs to his father, how he would have him called. [63] And he asked for a writing table, and wrote, saying, His name is John. And they marvelled all. [64] And his mouth was opened immediately, and his tongue *loosed*, and he spake, and praised God.

[65] And fear came on all that dwelt round about them: and all these sayings were noised abroad throughout all the hill country of Judaea. [66] And all they that heard *them* laid *them* up in their hearts, saying, What manner of child shall this be! And the hand of the Lord was with him.

[67] And his father Zacharias was filled with the Holy Ghost, and prophesied, saying, [68] Blessed *be* the Lord God of Israel; for he hath visited and redeemed his people, [69] and hath raised up an horn of salvation for us in the house of his servant David; [70] as he spake by the mouth of his holy prophets, which have been since the world began: [71] that we should be saved from our enemies, and from the hand of all that hate us; [72] to perform the mercy *promised* to our fathers, and to remember his holy covenant; [73] the oath which he sware to our father Abraham, [74] that he would grant unto us, that we being delivered out of the hand of our enemies might serve him without fear, [75] in holiness and righteousness before him, all the days of our life. [76] And thou, child, shalt be called the prophet of the Highest: for thou shalt go before the face of the Lord to prepare his ways; [77] to give knowledge of salvation unto his people by the remission of their sins, [78] through the tender mercy of our God; whereby the dayspring from on high hath visited us, [79] to give light to them that sit in darkness and *in* the shadow of death, to guide our feet into the way of peace.

[80] And the child grew, and

waxed strong in spirit, and was in the deserts till the day of his shewing unto Israel.

The birth and childhood of Jesus Christ

2 And it came to pass in those days, that there went out a decree from Caesar Augustus, that all the world should be taxed. ²(*And* this taxing was first made when Cyrenius was governor of Syria.) ³And all went to be taxed, every one into his own city.

⁴And Joseph also went up from Galilee, out of the city of Nazareth, into Judaea, unto the city of David, which is called Bethlehem; (because he was of the house and lineage of David:) ⁵to be taxed with Mary his espoused wife, being great with child.

⁶And so it was, that, while they were there, the days were accomplished that she should be delivered. ⁷And she brought forth her firstborn son, and wrapped him in swaddling clothes, and laid him in a manger; because there was no room for them in the inn.

⁸And there were in the same country shepherds abiding in the field, keeping watch over their flock by night. ⁹And, lo, the angel of the Lord came upon them, and the glory of the Lord shone round about them: and they were sore afraid. ¹⁰And the angel said unto them, Fear not: for, behold, I bring you good tidings of great joy, which shall be to all people. ¹¹For unto you is born this day in the city of David a Saviour, which is Christ the Lord. ¹²And this *shall be* a sign unto you; Ye shall find the babe wrapped in swaddling clothes, lying in a manger.

¹³And suddenly there was with the angel a multitude of the heavenly host praising God, and saying, ¹⁴Glory to God in the highest, and on earth peace, good will toward men.

¹⁵And it came to pass, as the angels were gone away from them into heaven, the shepherds said one to another, Let us now go even unto Bethlehem, and see this thing which is come to pass, which the Lord hath made known unto us. ¹⁶And they came with haste, and found Mary, and Joseph, and the babe lying in a manger. ¹⁷And when they had seen *it*, they made known abroad the saying which was told them concerning this child. ¹⁸And all they that heard *it* wondered at

those things which were told them by the shepherds. [19]But Mary kept all these things, and pondered *them* in her heart. [20]And the shepherds returned, glorifying and praising God for all the things that they had heard and seen, as it was told unto them.

[21]And when eight days were accomplished for the circumcising of the child, his name was called JESUS, which was so named of the angel before he was conceived in the womb. [22]And when the days of her purification according to the law of Moses were accomplished, they brought him to Jerusalem, to present *him* to the Lord; [23](as it is written in the law of the Lord, Every male that openeth the womb shall be called holy to the Lord;) [24]and to offer a sacrifice according to that which is said in the law of the Lord, A pair of turtledoves, or two young pigeons.

[25]And, behold, there was a man in Jerusalem, whose name *was* Simeon; and the same man *was* just and devout, waiting for the consolation of Israel: and the Holy Ghost was upon him. [26]And it was revealed unto him by the Holy Ghost, that he should not see death, before he had seen the Lord's Christ. [27]And he came by the Spirit into the temple: and when the parents brought in the child Jesus, to do for him after the custom of the law, [28]then took he him up in his arms, and blessed God, and said, [29]Lord, now lettest thou thy servant depart in peace, according to thy word: [30]for mine eyes have seen thy salvation, [31]which thou hast prepared before the face of all people; [32]a light to lighten the Gentiles, and the glory of thy people Israel.

[33]And Joseph and his mother marvelled at those things which were spoken of him. [34]And Simeon blessed them, and said unto Mary his mother, Behold, this *child* is set for the fall and rising again of many in Israel; and for a sign which shall be spoken against; [35](yea, a sword shall pierce through thy own soul also,) that the thoughts of many hearts may be revealed.

[36]And there was one Anna, a prophetess, the daughter of Phanuel, of the tribe of Aser: she was of a great age, and had lived with an husband seven years from her virginity; [37]and she *was* a widow of about fourscore and four years, which departed not from the temple, but served *God* with fastings and prayers night

and day. ³⁸And she coming in that instant gave thanks likewise unto the Lord, and spake of him to all them that looked for redemption in Jerusalem.

³⁹And when they had performed all things according to the law of the Lord, they returned into Galilee, to their own city Nazareth. ⁴⁰And the child grew, and waxed strong in spirit, filled with wisdom: and the grace of God was upon him.

⁴¹Now his parents went to Jerusalem every year at the feast of the passover. ⁴²And when he was twelve years old, they went up to Jerusalem after the custom of the feast. ⁴³And when they had fulfilled the days, as they returned, the child Jesus tarried behind in Jerusalem; and Joseph and his mother knew not *of it*. ⁴⁴But they, supposing him to have been in the company, went a day's journey; and they sought him among *their* kinsfolk and acquaintance. ⁴⁵And when they found him not, they turned back again to Jerusalem, seeking him. ⁴⁶And it came to pass, that after three days they found him in the temple, sitting in the midst of the doctors, both hearing them, and asking them questions. ⁴⁷And all that heard him were astonished at his understanding and answers.

⁴⁸And when they saw him, they were amazed: and his mother said unto him, Son, why hast thou thus dealt with us? behold, thy father and I have sought thee sorrowing. ⁴⁹And he said unto them, How is it that ye sought me? wist ye not that I must be about my Father's business? ⁵⁰And they understood not the saying which he spake unto them. ⁵¹And he went down with them, and came to Nazareth, and was subject unto them: but his mother kept all these sayings in her heart.

⁵²And Jesus increased in wisdom and stature, and in favour with God and man.

The ministry of John the Baptist

Matthew 3.1–12; Mark 1.1–8; John 1.15–31

3 Now in the fifteenth year of the reign of Tiberius Caesar, Pontius Pilate being governor of Judaea, and Herod being tetrarch of Galilee, and his brother Philip tetrarch of Ituraea and of the region of Trachonitis, and Lysanias the tetrarch of Abilene, ²Annas and Caiaphas being the high priests, the word of God came unto John the son of Zacharias in the wilderness. ³And he came into all the

country about Jordan, preaching the baptism of repentance for the remission of sins; [4]as it is written in the book of the words of Esaias the prophet, saying, The voice of one crying in the wilderness, Prepare ye the way of the Lord, make his paths straight. [5]Every valley shall be filled, and every mountain and hill shall be brought low; and the crooked *shall be* made straight, and the rough ways shall be made smooth; [6]and all flesh shall see the salvation of God.

[7]Then said he to the multitude that came forth to be baptized of him, O generation of vipers, who hath warned you to flee from the wrath to come? [8]Bring forth therefore fruits worthy of repentance, and begin not to say within yourselves, We have Abraham to *our* father: for I say unto you, That God is able of these stones to raise up children unto Abraham. [9]And now also the axe is laid unto the root of the trees: every tree therefore which bringeth not forth good fruit is hewn down, and cast into the fire.

[10]And the people asked him, saying, What shall we do then? [11]He answereth and saith unto them, He that hath two coats, let him impart to him that hath none; and he that hath meat, let him do likewise.

[12]Then came also publicans to be baptized, and said unto him, Master, what shall we do? [13]And he said unto them, Exact no more than that which is appointed you.

[14]And the soldiers likewise demanded of him, saying, And what shall we do? And he said unto them, Do violence to no man, neither accuse *any* falsely; and be content with your wages.

[15]And as the people were in expectation, and all men mused in their hearts of John, whether he were the Christ, or not; [16]John answered, saying unto *them* all, I indeed baptize you with water; but one mightier than I cometh, the latchet of whose shoes I am not worthy to unloose: he shall baptize you with the Holy Ghost and with fire: [17]whose fan *is* in his hand, and he will throughly purge his floor, and will gather the wheat into his garner; but the chaff he will burn with fire unquenchable.

[18]And many other things in his exhortation preached he unto the people. [19]But Herod the tetrarch, being reproved by him for Herodias his brother Philip's

wife, and for all the evils which Herod had done, 20added yet this above all, that he shut up John in prison.

The baptism and genealogy of Jesus
Matthew 1.1–16; 3.13–17; Mark 1.9–11; John 1.32–34

21Now when all the people were baptized, it came to pass, that Jesus also being baptized, and praying, the heaven was opened, 22and the Holy Ghost descended in a bodily shape like a dove upon him, and a voice came from heaven, which said, Thou art my beloved Son; in thee I am well pleased.

23And Jesus himself began to be about thirty years of age, being (as was supposed) the son of Joseph, which was *the son* of Heli, 24which was *the son* of Matthat, which was *the son* of Levi, which was *the son* of Melchi, which was *the son* of Janna, which was *the son* of Joseph, 25which was *the son* of Mattathias, which was *the son* of Amos, which was *the son* of Naum, which was *the son* of Esli, which was *the son* of Nagge, 26which was *the son* of Maath, which was *the son* of Mattathias, which was *the son* of Semei, which was *the son* of Joseph, which was *the son* of Juda, 27which was *the son* of Joanna, which was *the son* of Rhesa, which was *the son* of Zorobabel, which was *the son* of Salathiel, which was *the son* of Neri, 28which was *the son* of Melchi, which was *the son* of Addi, which was *the son* of Cosam, which was *the son* of Elmodam, which was *the son* of Er, 29which was *the son* of Jose, which was *the son* of Eliezer, which was *the son* of Jorim, which was *the son* of Matthat, which was *the son* of Levi, 30which was *the son* of Simeon, which was *the son* of Juda, which was *the son* of Joseph, which was *the son* of Jonan, which was *the son* of Eliakim, 31which was *the son* of Melea, which was *the son* of Menan, which was *the son* of Mattatha, which was *the son of* Nathan, which was *the son* of David, 32which was *the son* of Jesse, which was *the son* of Obed, which was *the son* of Booz, which was *the son* of Salmon, which was *the son* of Naasson, 33which was *the son* of Aminadab, which was *the son* of Aram, which was *the son* of Esrom, which was *the son* of Phares, which was *the son* of Juda, 34which was *the son* of Jacob, which was *the son* of Isaac, which was *the son* of Abraham, which was *the son* of Thara, which was *the son* of Nachor, ³⁵which was *the son* of Saruch, which was *the son* of Ragau, which was *the son* of Phalec, which was *the son* of Heber, which was *the son* of Sala, ³⁶which was *the son* of Cainan, which was *the son* of Arphaxad, which was *the son* of Sem, which was *the son* of Noe, which was *the son* of Lamech, ³⁷which was *the son* of Mathusala, which was *the son* of Enoch, which was *the son* of Jared, which was *the son* of Maleleel, which was *the son* of Cainan, ³⁸which was *the son* of Enos, which was *the son* of Seth, which was *the son* of Adam, which was *the son* of God.

The temptation in the wilderness

Matthew 4.1–11; Mark 1.12–13

And Jesus being full of the Holy Ghost returned from Jordan, and was led by the Spirit into the wilderness, ²being forty days tempted of the devil. And in those days he did eat nothing: and when they were ended, he afterward hungered. ³And the devil said unto him, If thou be the Son of God, command this stone that it be made bread. ⁴And Jesus answered him, saying, It is written, That man shall not live by bread alone, but by every word of God.

⁵And the devil, taking him up into an high mountain, shewed unto him all the kingdoms of the world in a moment of time. ⁶And the devil said unto him, All this power will I give thee, and the glory of them: for that is delivered unto me; and to whomsoever I will I give it. ⁷If thou therefore wilt worship me, all shall be thine. ⁸And Jesus answered and said unto him, Get thee behind me, Satan: for it is written, Thou shalt worship the Lord thy God, and him only shalt thou serve.

⁹And he brought him to Jerusalem, and set him on a pinnacle of the temple, and said unto him, If thou be the Son of God, cast thyself down from hence: ¹⁰for it is written, He shall give his angels charge over thee, to keep thee: ¹¹and in *their* hands they shall bear thee up, lest at any time thou dash thy foot against a stone. ¹²And Jesus answering said unto him, It is said, Thou shalt not tempt the Lord thy God.

¹³And when the devil had ended all the temptation, he departed from him for a season.

Jesus begins His ministry in Galilee and Nazareth

*Matthew 4.12–17; 13.53–58;
Mark 1.14, 15; 6.1–6*

14And Jesus returned in the power of the Spirit into Galilee: and there went out a fame of him through all the region round about. **15**And he taught in their synagogues, being glorified of all.

16And he came to Nazareth, where he had been brought up: and, as his custom was, he went into the synagogue on the sabbath day, and stood up for to read. **17**And there was delivered unto him the book of the prophet Esaias. And when he had opened the book, he found the place where it was written, **18**The Spirit of the Lord *is* upon me, because he hath anointed me to preach the gospel to the poor; he hath sent me to heal the brokenhearted, to preach deliverance to the captives, and recovering of sight to the blind, to set at liberty them that are bruised, **19**to preach the acceptable year of the Lord. **20**And he closed the book, and he gave *it* again to the minister, and sat down. And the eyes of all them that were in the synagogue were fastened on him.

21And he began to say unto them, This day is this scripture fulfilled in your ears. **22**And all bare him witness, and wondered at the gracious words which proceeded out of his mouth. And they said, Is not this Joseph's son? **23**And he said unto them, Ye will surely say unto me this proverb, Physician, heal thyself: whatsoever we have heard done in Capernaum, do also here in thy country. **24**And he said, Verily I say unto you, No prophet is accepted in his own country. **25**But I tell you of a truth, many widows were in Israel in the days of Elias, when the heaven was shut up three years and six months, when great famine was throughout all the land; **26**but unto none of them was Elias sent, save unto Sarepta, *a city* of Sidon, unto a woman *that was* a widow. **27**And many lepers were in Israel in the time of Eliseus the prophet; and none of them was cleansed, saving Naaman the Syrian.

28And all they in the synagogue, when they heard these things, were filled with wrath, **29**and rose up, and thrust him out of the city, and led him unto the brow of the hill whereon their city was built, that they might cast him down headlong.

At Capernaum. Miracles of healing

Matthew 8.14–17; Mark 1.21–39

30But he passing through the midst of them went his way, **31**and came down to Capernaum, a city of Galilee, and taught them on the sabbath days. **32**And they were astonished at his doctrine: for his word was with power.

33And in the synagogue there was a man, which had a spirit of an unclean devil, and cried out with a loud voice, **34**saying, Let *us* alone; what have we to do with thee, *thou* Jesus of Nazareth? art thou come to destroy us? I know thee who thou art; the Holy One of God. **35**And Jesus rebuked him, saying, Hold thy peace, and come out of him. And when the devil had thrown him in the midst, he came out of him, and hurt him not.

36And they were all amazed, and spake among themselves, saying, What a word *is* this! for with authority and power he commandeth the unclean spirits, and they come out. **37**And the fame of him went out into every place of the country round about.

38And he arose out of the synagogue, and entered into Simon's house. And Simon's wife's mother was taken with a great fever; and they besought him for her. **39**And he stood over her, and rebuked the fever; and it left her: and immediately she arose and ministered unto them.

40Now when the sun was setting, all they that had any sick with divers diseases brought them unto him; and he laid his hands on every one of them, and healed them. **41**And devils also came out of many, crying out, and saying, Thou art Christ the Son of God. And he rebuking *them* suffered them not to speak: for they knew that he was Christ.

42And when it was day, he departed and went into a desert place: and the people sought him, and came unto him, and stayed him, that he should not depart from them. **43**And he said unto them, I must preach the kingdom of God to other cities also: for therefore am I sent. **44**And he preached in the synagogues of Galilee.

The miraculous draught of fishes

5 And it came to pass, that, as the people pressed upon him to hear the word of

God, he stood by the lake of Gennesaret, 2and saw two ships standing by the lake: but the fishermen were gone out of them, and were washing *their* nets. 3And he entered into one of the ships, which was Simon's, and prayed him that he would thrust out a little from the land. And he sat down, and taught the people out of the ship.

4Now when he had left speaking, he said unto Simon, Launch out into the deep, and let down your nets for a draught. 5And Simon answering said unto him, Master, we have toiled all the night, and have taken nothing: nevertheless at thy word I will let down the net. 6And when they had this done, they inclosed a great multitude of fishes: and their net brake. 7And they beckoned unto *their* partners, which were in the other ship, that they should come and help them. And they came, and filled both the ships, so that they began to sink.

8When Simon Peter saw *it*, he fell down at Jesus' knees, saying, Depart from me; for I am a sinful man, O Lord. 9For he was astonished, and all that were with him, at the draught of the fishes which they had taken: 10and so *was* also James, and John, the sons of Zebedee, which were partners with Simon. And Jesus said unto Simon, Fear not; from henceforth thou shalt catch men. 11And when they had brought their ships to land, they forsook all, and followed him.

A leper cleansed and a paralytic healed

Matthew 8.1–4; 9.1–8; Mark 1.40–2.12

12And it came to pass, when he was in a certain city, behold a man full of leprosy: who seeing Jesus fell on *his* face, and besought him, saying, Lord, if thou wilt, thou canst make me clean. 13And he put forth *his* hand, and touched him, saying, I will: be thou clean. And immediately the leprosy departed from him. 14And he charged him to tell no man: but go, and shew thyself to the priest, and offer for thy cleansing, according as Moses commanded, for a testimony unto them.

15But so much the more went there a fame abroad of him: and great multitudes came together to hear, and to be healed by him of their infirmities. 16And he withdrew himself into the wilderness, and prayed.

17And it came to pass on a

certain day, as he was teaching, that there were Pharisees and doctors of the law sitting by, which were come out of every town of Galilee, and Judaea, and Jerusalem: and the power of the Lord was *present* to heal them. 18And, behold, men brought in a bed a man which was taken with a palsy: and they sought *means* to bring him in, and to lay *him* before him. 19And when they could not find by what *way* they might bring him in because of the multitude, they went upon the housetop, and let him down through the tiling with *his* couch into the midst before Jesus. 20And when he saw their faith, he said unto him, Man, thy sins are forgiven thee. 21And the scribes and the Pharisees began to reason, saying, Who is this which speaketh blasphemies? Who can forgive sins, but God alone?

22But when Jesus perceived their thoughts, he answering said unto them, What reason ye in your hearts? 23Whether is easier, to say, Thy sins be forgiven thee; or to say, Rise up and walk? 24But that ye may know that the Son of man hath power upon earth to forgive sins, (he said unto the sick of the palsy,) I say unto thee, Arise, and take up thy couch, and go into thine house. 25And immediately he rose up before them, and took up that whereon he lay, and departed to his own house, glorifying God. 26And they were all amazed, and they glorified God, and were filled with fear, saying, We have seen strange things to day.

The calling of Levi
Matthew 9.9–13; Mark 2.13–17

27And after these things he went forth, and saw a publican, named Levi, sitting at the receipt of custom: and he said unto him, Follow me. 28And he left all, rose up, and followed him.

29And Levi made him a great feast in his own house: and there was a great company of publicans and of others that sat down with them. 30But their scribes and Pharisees murmured against his disciples, saying, Why do ye eat and drink with publicans and sinners? 31And Jesus answering said unto them, They that are whole need not a physician; but they that are sick. 32I came not to call the righteous, but sinners to repentance.

33And they said unto him, Why do the disciples of John fast often, and make prayers, and likewise *the disciples* of the Pharisees; but thine eat and drink? 34And he said unto them,

Can ye make the children of the bridechamber fast, while the bridegroom is with them? 35But the days will come, when the bridegroom shall be taken away from them, and then shall they fast in those days.

36And he spake also a parable unto them; No man putteth a piece of a new garment upon an old; if otherwise, then both the new maketh a rent, and the piece that was *taken* out of the new agreeth not with the old. 37And no man putteth new wine into old bottles; else the new wine will burst the bottles, and be spilled, and the bottles shall perish. 38But new wine must be put into new bottles; and both are preserved. 39No man also having drunk old *wine* straightway desireth new: for he saith, The old is better.

Jesus and the sabbath

Matthew 12.1–14; Mark 2.23–3.6

6And it came to pass on the second sabbath after the first, that he went through the corn fields; and his disciples plucked the ears of corn, and did eat, rubbing *them* in *their* hands. 2And certain of the Pharisees said unto them, Why do ye that which is not lawful to do on the sabbath days?

3And Jesus answering them said, Have ye not read so much as this, what David did, when himself was an hungred, and they which were with him; 4how he went into the house of God, and did take and eat the shewbread, and gave also to them that were with him; which it is not lawful to eat but for the priests alone? 5And he said unto them, That the Son of man is Lord also of the sabbath.

6And it came to pass also on another sabbath, that he entered into the synagogue and taught: and there was a man whose right hand was withered. 7And the scribes and Pharisees watched him, whether he would heal on the sabbath day; that they might find an accusation against him. 8But he knew their thoughts, and said to the man which had the withered hand, Rise up, and stand forth in the midst. And he arose and stood forth. 9Then said Jesus unto them, I will ask you one thing; Is it lawful on the sabbath days to do good, or to do evil? to save life, or to destroy *it*? 10And looking round about upon them all, he said unto the man, Stretch forth thy hand. And he did so: and his hand was restored whole as the other.

11And they were filled with

madness; and communed one with another what they might do to Jesus.

Jesus chooses and teaches the twelve apostles

Matthew 10.1–4; Mark 3.13–19

12 And it came to pass in those days, that he went out into a mountain to pray, and continued all night in prayer to God. 13And when it was day, he called *unto him* his disciples: and of them he chose twelve, whom also he named apostles; 14Simon, (whom he also named Peter,) and Andrew his brother, James and John, Philip and Bartholomew, 15Matthew and Thomas, James the *son* of Alphaeus, and Simon called Zelotes, 16and Judas *the brother* of James, and Judas Iscariot, which also was the traitor.

17And he came down with them, and stood in the plain, and the company of his disciples, and a great multitude of people out of all Judaea and Jerusalem, and from the sea coast of Tyre and Sidon, which came to hear him, and to be healed of their diseases; 18and they that were vexed with unclean spirits: and they were healed. 19And the whole multitude sought to touch him: for there went virtue out of him, and healed *them* all.

20And he lifted up his eyes on his disciples, and said, Blessed *be ye* poor: for yours is the kingdom of God.

21Blessed *are ye* that hunger now: for ye shall be filled. Blessed *are ye* that weep now: for ye shall laugh.

22Blessed are ye, when men shall hate you, and when they shall separate you *from their company*, and shall reproach *you*, and cast out your name as evil, for the Son of man's sake. 23Rejoice ye in that day, and leap for joy: for, behold, your reward *is* great in heaven: for in the like manner did their fathers unto the prophets.

24But woe unto you that are rich! for ye have received your consolation.

25Woe unto you that are full! for ye shall hunger. Woe unto you that laugh now! for ye shall mourn and weep.

26Woe unto you, when all men shall speak well of you! for so did their fathers to the false prophets.

27But I say unto you which hear, Love your enemies, do

good to them which hate you, 28bless them that curse you, and pray for them which despitefully use you. 29And unto him that smiteth thee on the *one* cheek offer also the other; and him that taketh away thy cloke forbid not *to take thy* coat also. 30Give to every man that asketh of thee; and of him that taketh away thy goods ask *them* not again. 31And as ye would that men should do to you, do ye also to them likewise. 32For if ye love them which love you, what thank have ye? for sinners also love those that love them. 33And if ye do good to them which do good to you, what thank have ye? for sinners also do even the same. 34And if ye lend *to them* of whom ye hope to receive, what thank have ye? for sinners also lend to sinners, to receive as much again. 35But love ye your enemies, and do good, and lend, hoping for nothing again; and your reward shall be great, and ye shall be the children of the Highest: for he is kind unto the unthankful and *to* the evil. 36Be ye therefore merciful, as your Father also is merciful.

37Judge not, and ye shall not be judged: condemn not, and ye shall not be condemned: forgive, and ye shall be forgiven: 38give, and it shall be given unto you;

good measure, pressed down, and shaken together, and running over, shall men give into your bosom. For with the same measure that ye mete withal it shall be measured to you again.

39And he spake a parable unto them, Can the blind lead the blind? shall they not both fall into the ditch? 40The disciple is not above his master: but every one that is perfect shall be as his master. 41And why beholdest thou the mote that is in thy brother's eye, but perceivest not the beam that is in thine own eye? 42Either how canst thou say to thy brother, Brother, let me pull out the mote that is in thine eye, when thou thyself beholdest not the beam that is in thine own eye? Thou hypocrite, cast out first the beam out of thine own eye, and then shalt thou see clearly to pull out the mote that is in thy brother's eye.

43 For a good tree bringeth not forth corrupt fruit; neither doth a corrupt tree bring forth good fruit. 44For every tree is known by his own fruit. For of thorns men do not gather figs, nor of a bramble bush gather they grapes. 45A good man out of the good treasure of his heart bringeth forth that which is good; and an evil man out of the evil treasure

of his heart bringeth forth that which is evil: for of the abundance of the heart his mouth speaketh.

46And why call ye me, Lord, Lord, and do not the things which I say? **47**Whosoever cometh to me, and heareth my sayings, and doeth them, I will shew you to whom he is like: **48**he is like a man which built an house, and digged deep, and laid the foundation on a rock: and when the flood arose, the stream beat vehemently upon that house, and could not shake it: for it was founded upon a rock. **49**But he that heareth, and doeth not, is like a man that without a foundation built an house upon the earth; against which the stream did beat vehemently, and immediately it fell; and the ruin of that house was great.

A centurion's servant healed and a dead man raised to life

7 Now when he had ended all his sayings in the audience of the people, he entered into Capernaum.

2And a certain centurion's servant, who was dear unto him, was sick, and ready to die. **3**And when he heard of Jesus, he sent unto him the elders of the Jews, beseeching him that he would come and heal his servant. **4**And when they came to Jesus, they besought him instantly, saying, That he was worthy for whom he should do this: **5**for he loveth our nation, and he hath built us a synagogue.

6Then Jesus went with them. And when he was now not far from the house, the centurion sent friends to him, saying unto him, Lord, trouble not thyself: for I am not worthy that thou shouldest enter under my roof: **7**wherefore neither thought I myself worthy to come unto thee: but say in a word, and my servant shall be healed. **8**For I also am a man set under authority, having under me soldiers, and I say unto one, Go, and he goeth; and to another, Come, and he cometh; and to my servant, Do this, and he doeth *it*.

9When Jesus heard these things, he marvelled at him, and turned him about, and said unto the people that followed him, I say unto you, I have not found so great faith, no, not in Israel. **10**And they that were sent, returning to the house, found the servant whole that had been sick.

11And it came to pass the day after, that he went into a city called Nain; and many of his disciples went with him, and much people. 12Now when he came nigh to the gate of the city, behold, there was a dead man carried out, the only son of his mother, and she was a widow: and much people of the city was with her. 13And when the Lord saw her, he had compassion on her, and said unto her, Weep not. 14And he came and touched the bier: and they that bare *him* stood still. And he said, Young man, I say unto thee, Arise. 15And he that was dead sat up, and began to speak. And he delivered him to his mother.

16And there came a fear on all: and they glorified God, saying, That a great prophet is risen up among us; and, That God hath visited his people. 17And this rumour of him went forth throughout all Judaea, and throughout all the region round about.

Jesus and John the Baptist

Matthew 11.2–19

18And the disciples of John shewed him of all these things. 19And John calling *unto him* two of his disciples sent *them* to Jesus, saying, Art thou he that should come? or look we for another?

20When the men were come unto him, they said, John Baptist hath sent us unto thee, saying, Art thou he that should come? or look we for another? 21And in that same hour he cured many of *their* infirmities and plagues, and of evil spirits; and unto many *that were* blind he gave sight. 22Then Jesus answering said unto them, Go your way, and tell John what things ye have seen and heard; how that the blind see, the lame walk, the lepers are cleansed, the deaf hear, the dead are raised, to the poor the gospel is preached. 23And blessed is *he*, whosoever shall not be offended in me.

24And when the messengers of John were departed, he began to speak unto the people concerning John, What went ye out into the wilderness for to see? A reed shaken with the wind? 25But what went ye out for to see? A man clothed in soft raiment? Behold, they which are gorgeously apparelled, and live delicately, are in kings' courts. 26But what went ye out for to see? A prophet? Yea, I say unto you, and much more than a prophet. 27This is *he*, of whom it is written, Behold, I send my messenger before thy face, which shall prepare thy way before thee.

28For I say unto you, Among

those that are born of women there is not a greater prophet than John the Baptist: but he that is least in the kingdom of God is greater than he. ²⁹And all the people that heard *him*, and the publicans, justified God, being baptized with the baptism of John. ³⁰But the Pharisees and lawyers rejected the counsel of God against themselves, being not baptized of him.

³¹And the Lord said, Whereunto then shall I liken the men of this generation? and to what are they like? ³²They are like unto children sitting in the marketplace, and calling one to another, and saying, We have piped unto you, and ye have not danced; we have mourned to you, and ye have not wept. ³³For John the Baptist came neither eating bread nor drinking wine; and ye say, He hath a devil. ³⁴The Son of man is come eating and drinking; and ye say, Behold a gluttonous man, and a winebibber, a friend of publicans and sinners! ³⁵But wisdom is justified of all her children.

A repentant sinner pardoned

³⁶And one of the Pharisees desired him that he would eat with him. And he went into the Pharisee's house, and sat down to meat. ³⁷And, behold, a woman in the city, which was a sinner, when she knew that *Jesus* sat at meat in the Pharisee's house, brought an alabaster box of ointment, ³⁸and stood at his feet behind *him* weeping, and began to wash his feet with tears, and did wipe *them* with the hairs of her head, and kissed his feet, and anointed *them* with the ointment. ³⁹Now when the Pharisee which had bidden him saw *it*, he spake within himself, saying, This man, if he were a prophet, would have known who and what manner of woman *this is* that toucheth him: for she is a sinner.

⁴⁰And Jesus answering said unto him, Simon, I have somewhat to say unto thee. And he saith, Master, say on. ⁴¹There was a certain creditor which had two debtors: the one owed five hundred pence, and the other fifty. ⁴²And when they had nothing to pay, he frankly forgave them both. Tell me therefore, which of them will love him most? ⁴³Simon answered and said, I suppose that *he*, to whom he forgave most. And he said unto him, Thou hast rightly judged.

⁴⁴And he turned to the

woman, and said unto Simon, Seest thou this woman? I entered into thine house, thou gavest me no water for my feet: but she hath washed my feet with tears, and wiped *them* with the hairs of her head. ⁴⁵Thou gavest me no kiss: but this woman since the time I came in hath not ceased to kiss my feet. ⁴⁶My head with oil thou didst not anoint: but this woman hath anointed my feet with ointment. ⁴⁷Wherefore I say unto thee, Her sins, which are many, are forgiven; for she loved much: but to whom little is forgiven, *the same* loveth little. ⁴⁸And he said unto her, Thy sins are forgiven.

⁴⁹And they that sat at meat with him began to say within themselves, Who is this that forgiveth sins also? ⁵⁰And he said to the woman, Thy faith hath saved thee; go in peace.

8 And it came to pass afterward, that he went throughout every city and village, preaching and shewing the glad tidings of the kingdom of God: and the twelve *were* with him, ²and certain women, which had been healed of evil spirits and infirmities, Mary called Magdalene, out of whom went seven devils, ³and Joanna the wife of Chuza Herod's steward, and Susanna, and many others, which ministered unto him of their substance.

The parable of the sower
Matthew 13.1–23; Mark 4.1–20

⁴And when much people were gathered together, and were come to him out of every city, he spake by a parable: ⁵A sower went out to sow his seed: and as he sowed, some fell by the way side; and it was trodden down, and the fowls of the air devoured it. ⁶And some fell upon a rock; and as soon as it was sprung up, it withered away, because it lacked moisture. ⁷And some fell among thorns; and the thorns sprang up with it, and choked it. ⁸And other fell on good ground, and sprang up, and bare fruit an hundredfold. And when he had said these things, he cried, He that hath ears to hear, let him hear.

⁹And his disciples asked him, saying, What might this parable be? ¹⁰And he said, Unto you it is given to know the mysteries of the kingdom of God: but to others in parables; that seeing they might not see, and hearing they might not understand.

¹¹Now the parable is this: The seed is the word of God. ¹²Those by the way side are they that hear; then cometh the devil, and taketh away the word out of their hearts, lest they should believe and be saved. 13They on the rock *are they*, which, when they hear, receive the word with joy; and these have no root, which for a while believe, and in time of temptation fall away. 14And that which fell among thorns are they, which, when they have heard, go forth, and are choked with cares and riches and pleasures of *this* life, and bring no fruit to perfection. 15But that on the good ground are they, which in an honest and good heart, having heard the word, keep *it*, and bring forth fruit with patience.

16No man, when he hath lighted a candle, covereth it with a vessel, or putteth *it* under a bed; but setteth *it* on a candlestick, that they which enter in may see the light. 17For nothing is secret, that shall not be made manifest; neither *any thing* hid, that shall not be known and come abroad. 18Take heed therefore how ye hear: for whosoever hath, to him shall be given; and whosoever hath not, from him shall be taken even that which he seemeth to have.

19Then came to him *his* mother and his brethren, and could not come at him for the press. 20And it was told him *by certain* which said, Thy mother and thy brethren stand without, desiring to see thee. 21And he answered and said unto them, My mother and my brethren are these which hear the word of God, and do it.

The storm stilled and devils cast out

Matthew 8.23–34; Mark 4.35–5.20

22Now it came to pass on a certain day, that he went into a ship with his disciples: and he said unto them, Let us go over unto the other side of the lake. And they launched forth. 23But as they sailed he fell asleep: and there came down a storm of wind on the lake; and they were filled *with water*, and were in jeopardy. 24And they came to him, and awoke him, saying, Master, master, we perish. Then he arose, and rebuked the wind and the raging of the water: and they ceased, and there was a calm. 25And he said unto them, Where is your faith? And they being afraid wondered, saying one to another, What manner of man is this! for he commandeth even the winds and water, and they obey him.

26And they arrived at the country of the Gadarenes, which is over against Galilee. 27And when he went forth to land, there met him out of the city a certain man, which had devils long time, and ware no clothes, neither abode in *any* house, but in the tombs. 28When he saw Jesus, he cried out, and fell down before him, and with a loud voice said, What have I to do with thee, Jesus, *thou* Son of God most high? I beseech thee, torment me not. 29(For he had commanded the unclean spirit to come out of the man. For oftentimes it had caught him: and he was kept bound with chains and in fetters; and he brake the bands, and was driven of the devil into the wilderness.)

30And Jesus asked him, saying, What is thy name? And he said, Legion: because many devils were entered into him. 31And they besought him that he would not command them to go out into the deep. 32And there was there an herd of many swine feeding on the mountain: and they besought him that he would suffer them to enter into them. And he suffered them. 33Then went the devils out of the man, and entered into the swine: and the herd ran violently down a steep place into the lake, and were choked.

34When they that fed *them* saw what was done, they fled, and went and told *it* in the city and in the country. 35Then they went out to see what was done; and came to Jesus, and found the man, out of whom the devils were departed, sitting at the feet of Jesus, clothed, and in his right mind: and they were afraid. 36They also which saw *it* told them by what means he that was possessed of the devils was healed. 37Then the whole multitude of the country of the Gadarenes round about besought him to depart from them; for they were taken with great fear: and he went up into the ship, and returned back again.

38Now the man out of whom the devils were departed besought him that he might be with him: but Jesus sent him away, saying, 39Return to thine own house, and shew how great things God hath done unto thee. And he went his way, and published throughout the whole city how great things Jesus had done unto him.

A child raised from the dead and a woman healed

Matthew 9.18–26; Mark 5.21–43

40And it came to pass, that,

when Jesus was returned, the people *gladly* received him: for they were all waiting for him. [41]And, behold, there came a man named Jairus, and he was a ruler of the synagogue: and he fell down at Jesus' feet, and besought him that he would come into his house: [42]for he had one only daughter, about twelve years of age, and she lay a dying. But as he went the people thronged him.

[43]And a woman having an issue of blood twelve years, which had spent all her living upon physicians, neither could be healed of any, [44]came behind *him*, and touched the border of his garment: and immediately her issue of blood stanched. [45]And Jesus said, Who touched me? When all denied, Peter and they that were with him said, Master, the multitude throng thee and press *thee*, and sayest thou, Who touched me? [46]And Jesus said, Somebody hath touched me: for I perceive that virtue is gone out of me. [47]And when the woman saw that she was not hid, she came trembling, and falling down before him, she declared unto him before all the people for what cause she had touched him, and how she was healed immediately. [48]And he said unto her, Daughter, be of good comfort: thy faith hath made thee whole; go in peace.

[49]While he yet spake, there cometh one from the ruler of the synagogue's *house*, saying to him, Thy daughter is dead; trouble not the Master. [50]But when Jesus heard *it*, he answered him, saying, Fear not: believe only, and she shall be made whole. [51]And when he came into the house, he suffered no man to go in, save Peter, and James, and John, and the father and the mother of the maiden. [52]And all wept, and bewailed her: but he said, Weep not; she is not dead, but sleepeth. [53]And they laughed him to scorn, knowing that she was dead. [54]And he put them all out, and took her by the hand, and called, saying, Maid, arise. [55]And her spirit came again, and she arose straightway: and he commanded to give her meat. [56]And her parents were astonished: but he charged them that they should tell no man what was done.

The twelve sent forth
Matthew 10.1–14; Mark 6.7–13

9 Then he called his twelve disciples together, and gave them power and authority over all devils, and to cure diseases. [2]And he sent them to preach the kingdom of God, and to heal the sick. [3]And he said unto them, Take nothing for *your*

journey, neither staves, nor scrip, neither bread, neither money; neither have two coats apiece. ⁴And whatsoever house ye enter into, there abide, and thence depart. ⁵And whosoever will not receive you, when ye go out of that city, shake off the very dust from your feet for a testimony against them. ⁶And they departed, and went through the towns, preaching the gospel, and healing every where.

Herod and Jesus. The feeding of five thousand

Matthew 14.1, 2, 13–21; Mark 6.14–16, 30–44; John 6.1–13

⁷Now Herod the tetrarch heard of all that was done by him: and he was perplexed, because that it was said of some, that John was risen from the dead; ⁸and of some, that Elias had appeared; and of others, that one of the old prophets was risen again. ⁹And Herod said, John have I beheaded: but who is this, of whom I hear such things? And he desired to see him.

¹⁰And the apostles, when they were returned, told him all that they had done. And he took them, and went aside privately into a desert place belonging to the city called Bethsaida. ¹¹And the people, when they knew *it*, followed him: and he received them, and spake unto them of the kingdom of God, and healed them that had need of healing.

¹²And when the day began to wear away, then came the twelve, and said unto him, Send the multitude away, that they may go into the towns and country round about, and lodge, and get victuals: for we are here in a desert place. ¹³But he said unto them, Give ye them to eat. And they said, We have no more but five loaves and two fishes; except we should go and buy meat for all this people. ¹⁴For they were about five thousand men. And he said to his disciples, Make them sit down by fifties in a company. ¹⁵And they did so, and made them all sit down. ¹⁶Then he took the five loaves and the two fishes, and looking up to heaven, he blessed them, and brake, and gave to the disciples to set before the multitude. ¹⁷And they did eat, and were all filled: and there was taken up of fragments that remained to them twelve baskets.

Peter's confession. Jesus foretells His death

Matthew 16.13–28; Mark 8.27–9.1

¹⁸And it came to pass, as he was alone praying, his disciples

were with him: and he asked them, saying, Whom say the people that I am? ¹⁹They answering said, John the Baptist; but some *say*, Elias; and others *say*, that one of the old prophets is risen again. ²⁰He said unto them, But whom say ye that I am? Peter answering said, The Christ of God. ²¹And he straitly charged them, and commanded *them* to tell no man that thing; ²²saying, The Son of man must suffer many things, and be rejected of the elders and chief priests and scribes, and be slain, and be raised the third day.

²³And he said to *them* all, If any *man* will come after me, let him deny himself, and take up his cross daily, and follow me. ²⁴For whosoever will save his life shall lose it: but whosoever will lose his life for my sake, the same shall save it. ²⁵For what is a man advantaged, if he gain the whole world, and lose himself, or be cast away? ²⁶For whosoever shall be ashamed of me and of my words, of him shall the Son of man be ashamed, when he shall come in his own glory, and *in his* Father's, and of the holy angels. ²⁷But I tell you of a truth, there be some standing here, which shall not taste of death, till they see the kingdom of God.

The transfiguration

Matthew 17.1–8; Mark 9.2–8

²⁸And it came to pass about an eight days after these sayings, he took Peter and John and James, and went up into a mountain to pray. ²⁹And as he prayed, the fashion of his countenance was altered, and his raiment *was* white *and* glistering. ³⁰And, behold, there talked with him two men, which were Moses and Elias: ³¹who appeared in glory, and spake of his decease which he should accomplish at Jerusalem.

³²But Peter and they that were with him were heavy with sleep: and when they were awake, they saw his glory, and the two men that stood with him. ³³And it came to pass, as they departed from him, Peter said unto Jesus, Master, it is good for us to be here: and let us make three tabernacles; one for thee, and one for Moses, and one for Elias: not knowing what he said. ³⁴While he thus spake, there came a cloud, and overshadowed them: and they feared as they entered into the cloud. ³⁵And there came a voice out of the cloud, saying, This is my beloved Son: hear him. ³⁶And when the voice was past, Jesus was found alone. And they kept *it* close, and

told no man in those days any of those things which they had seen.

A devil cast out

Matthew 17.14–21; Mark 9.14–29

37And it came to pass, that on the next day, when they were come down from the hill, much people met him. **38** And, behold, a man of the company cried out, saying, Master, I beseech thee, look upon my son: for he is mine only child. **39**And, lo, a spirit taketh him, and he suddenly crieth out; and it teareth him that he foameth again, and bruising him hardly departeth from him. **40**And I besought thy disciples to cast him out; and they could not. **41**And Jesus answering said, O faithless and perverse generation, how long shall I be with you, and suffer you? Bring thy son hither. **42**And as he was yet a coming, the devil threw him down, and *tare* him. And Jesus rebuked the unclean spirit, and healed the child, and delivered him again to his father.

Jesus again foretells His coming death

Matthew 17.22, 23; Mark 9.30–32

43And they were all amazed at the mighty power of God. But while they wondered every one at all things which Jesus did, he said unto his disciples, **44**Let these sayings sink down into your ears: for the Son of man shall be delivered into the hands of men. **45**But they understood not this saying, and it was hid from them, that they perceived it not: and they feared to ask him of that saying.

46Then there arose a reasoning among them, which of them should be greatest. **47**And Jesus, perceiving the thought of their heart, took a child, and set him by him, **48**and said unto them, Whosoever shall receive this child in my name receiveth me: and whosoever shall receive me receiveth him that sent me: for he that is least among you all, the same shall be great.

49And John answered and said, Master, we saw one casting out devils in thy name; and we forbad *him*, because he followeth not with us. **50**And Jesus said unto him, Forbid *him* not: for he that is not against us is for us.

51And it came to pass, when the time was come that he should be received up, he stedfastly set his face to go to Jerusalem, **52**and sent messengers before his face: and they went, and entered into a village of the

Samaritans, to make ready for him. ⁵³And they did not receive him, because his face was as though he would go to Jerusalem.

⁵⁴And when his disciples James and John saw *this*, they said, Lord, wilt thou that we command fire to come down from heaven, and consume them, even as Elias did? ⁵⁵But he turned, and rebuked them, and said, Ye know not what manner of spirit ye are of. ⁵⁶For the Son of man is not come to destroy men's lives, but to save *them*. And they went to another village.

⁵⁷And it came to pass, that, as they went in the way, a certain *man* said unto him, Lord, I will follow thee whithersoever thou goest. ⁵⁸And Jesus said unto him, Foxes have holes, and birds of the air *have* nests; but the Son of man hath not where to lay *his* head. ⁵⁹And he said unto another, Follow me. But he said, Lord, suffer me first to go and bury my father. ⁶⁰Jesus said unto him, Let the dead bury their dead: but go thou and preach the kingdom of God. ⁶¹And another also said, Lord, I will follow thee; but let me first go bid them farewell, which are at home at my house. ⁶²And Jesus said unto him, No man, having put his hand to the plough, and looking back, is fit for the kingdom of God.

Seventy disciples sent out

10 After these things the Lord appointed other seventy also, and sent them two and two before his face into every city and place, whither he himself would come. ²Therefore said he unto them, The harvest truly *is* great, but the labourers *are* few: pray ye therefore the Lord of the harvest, that he would send forth labourers into his harvest.

³Go your ways: behold, I send you forth as lambs among wolves. ⁴Carry neither purse, nor scrip, nor shoes: and salute no man by the way. ⁵And into whatsoever house ye enter, first say, Peace *be* to this house. ⁶And if the son of peace be there, your peace shall rest upon it: if not, it shall turn to you again. ⁷And in the same house remain, eating and drinking such things as they give: for the labourer is worthy of his hire. Go not from house to house.

⁸And into whatsoever city ye enter, and they receive you, eat such things as are set before you:

[9]and heal the sick that are therein, and say unto them, The kingdom of God is come nigh unto you. [10]But into whatsoever city ye enter, and they receive you not, go your ways out into the streets of the same, and say, [11]Even the very dust of your city, which cleaveth on us, we do wipe off against you: notwithstanding be ye sure of this, that the kingdom of God is come nigh unto you. [12]But I say unto you, that it shall be more tolerable in that day for Sodom, than for that city.

[13]Woe unto thee, Chorazin! woe unto thee, Bethsaida! for if the mighty works had been done in Tyre and Sidon, which have been done in you, they had a great while ago repented, sitting in sackcloth and ashes. [14]But it shall be more tolerable for Tyre and Sidon at the judgment, than for you. [15]And thou, Capernaum, which art exalted to heaven, shalt be thrust down to hell.

[16]He that heareth you heareth me; and he that despiseth you despiseth me; and he that despiseth me despiseth him that sent me.

[17]And the seventy returned again with joy, saying, Lord, even the devils are subject unto us through thy name. [18]And he said unto them, I beheld Satan as lightning fall from heaven. [19]Behold, I give unto you power to tread on serpents and scorpions, and over all the power of the enemy: and nothing shall by any means hurt you. [20]Notwithstanding in this rejoice not, that the spirits are subject unto you; but rather rejoice, because your names are written in heaven.

[21]In that hour Jesus rejoiced in spirit, and said, I thank thee, O Father, Lord of heaven and earth, that thou hast hid these things from the wise and prudent, and hast revealed them unto babes: even so, Father; for so it seemed good in thy sight. [22]All things are delivered to me of my Father: and no man knoweth who the Son is, but the Father; and who the Father is, but the Son, and *he* to whom the Son will reveal *him*.

[23]And he turned him unto *his* disciples, and said privately, Blessed *are* the eyes which see the things that ye see: [24]for I tell you, that many prophets and kings have desired to see those things which ye see, and have not seen *them*; and to hear those things which ye hear, and have not heard *them*.

The great commandment. Parable of the good Samaritan

Matthew 22.35–40; Mark 12.28–34

25And, behold, a certain lawyer stood up, and tempted him, saying, Master, what shall I do to inherit eternal life? 26He said unto him, What is written in the law? how readest thou? 27And he answering said, Thou shalt love the Lord thy God with all thy heart, and with all thy soul, and with all thy strength, and with all thy mind; and thy neighbour as thyself. 28And he said unto him, Thou hast answered right: this do, and thou shalt live. 29But he, willing to justify himself, said unto Jesus, And who is my neighbour?

30And Jesus answering said, A certain *man* went down from Jerusalem to Jericho, and fell among thieves, which stripped him of his raiment, and wounded *him*, and departed, leaving *him* half dead. 31And by chance there came down a certain priest that way: and when he saw him, he passed by on the other side. 32And likewise a Levite, when he was at the place, came and looked *on him*, and passed by on the other side. 33But a certain Samaritan, as he journeyed, came where he was: and when he saw him, he had compassion *on him*, 34and went to *him*, and bound up his wounds, pouring in oil and wine, and set him on his own beast, and brought him to an inn, and took care of him. 35And on the morrow when he departed, he took out two pence, and gave *them* to the host, and said unto him, Take care of him; and whatsoever thou spendest more, when I come again, I will repay thee. 36Which now of these three, thinkest thou, was neighbour unto him that fell among the thieves? 37And he said, He that shewed mercy on him. Then said Jesus unto him, Go, and do thou likewise.

38Now it came to pass, as they went, that he entered into a certain village: and a certain woman named Martha received him into her house. 39And she had a sister called Mary, which also sat at Jesus' feet, and heard his word. 40But Martha was cumbered about much serving, and came to him, and said, Lord, dost thou not care that my sister hath left me to serve alone? bid her therefore that she help me. 41And Jesus answered and said unto her, Martha, Martha, thou art careful and troubled about many things: 42but one thing is needful: and Mary hath chosen that good part, which shall not be taken away from her.

Teaching on prayer

Matthew 6.9–13

11 And it came to pass, that, as he was praying in a certain place, when he ceased, one of his disciples said unto him, Lord, teach us to pray, as John also taught his disciples.

2And he said unto them, When ye pray, say, Our Father which art in heaven, Hallowed be thy name. Thy kingdom come. Thy will be done, as in heaven, so in earth. ³Give us day by day our daily bread. ⁴And forgive us our sins; for we also forgive every one that is indebted to us. And lead us not into temptation; but deliver us from evil.

5And he said unto them, Which of you shall have a friend, and shall go unto him at midnight, and say unto him, Friend, lend me three loaves; ⁶for a friend of mine in his journey is come to me, and I have nothing to set before him? ⁷And he from within shall answer and say, Trouble me not: the door is now shut, and my children are with me in bed; I cannot rise and give thee. ⁸I say unto you, Though he will not rise and give him, because he is his friend, yet because of his importunity he will rise and give him as many as he needeth.

9And I say unto you, Ask, and it shall be given you; seek, and ye shall find; knock, and it shall be opened unto you. ¹⁰For every one that asketh receiveth; and he that seeketh findeth; and to him that knocketh it shall be opened. ¹¹If a son shall ask bread of any of you that is a father, will he give him a stone? or if *he ask* a fish, will he for a fish give him a serpent? ¹²Or if he shall ask an egg, will he offer him a scorpion? ¹³If ye then, being evil, know how to give good gifts unto your children: how much more shall *your* heavenly Father give the Holy Spirit to them that ask him?

The power of Jesus over evil spirits

Matthew 12.22–30, 43–45; Mark 3.22–27

14And he was casting out a devil, and it was dumb. And it came to pass, when the devil was gone out, the dumb spake; and the people wondered. ¹⁵But some of them said, He casteth out devils through Beelzebub the chief of the devils. [16]And others, tempting *him*, sought of him a sign from heaven.

[17]But he, knowing their thoughts, said unto them, Every kingdom divided against itself is brought to desolation; and a house *divided* against a house falleth. [18]If Satan also be divided against himself, how shall his kingdom stand? because ye say that I cast out devils through Beelzebub. [19]And if I by Beelzebub cast out devils, by whom do your sons cast *them* out? therefore shall they be your judges. [20]But if I with the finger of God cast out devils, no doubt the kingdom of God is come upon you.

[21]When a strong man armed keepeth his palace, his goods are in peace: [22]but when a stronger than he shall come upon him, and overcome him, he taketh from him all his armour wherein he trusted, and divideth his spoils. [23]He that is not with me is against me: and he that gathereth not with me scattereth. [24]When the unclean spirit is gone out of a man, he walketh through dry places, seeking rest; and finding none, he saith, I will return unto my house whence I came out. [25]And when he cometh, he findeth *it* swept and garnished.

[26]Then goeth he, and taketh *to him* seven other spirits more wicked than himself; and they enter in, and dwell there: and the last *state* of that man is worse than the first.

[27]And it came to pass, as he spake these things, a certain woman of the company lifted up her voice, and said unto him, Blessed *is* the womb that bare thee, and the paps which thou hast sucked. [28]But he said, Yea rather, blessed *are* they that hear the word of God, and keep it.

[29]And when the people were gathered thick together, he began to say, This is an evil generation: they seek a sign; and there shall no sign be given it, but the sign of Jonas the prophet. [30]For as Jonas was a sign unto the Ninevites, so shall also the Son of man be to this generation. [31]The queen of the south shall rise up in the judgment with the men of this generation, and condemn them: for she came from the utmost parts of the earth to hear the wisdom of Solomon; and, behold, a greater than Solomon *is* here. [32]The men of Nineve shall rise up in the judgment with this generation, and shall condemn it: for they repented at the preaching of Jonas; and, behold, a greater than Jonas *is* here.

33No man, when he hath lighted a candle, putteth *it* in a secret place, neither under a bushel, but on a candlestick, that they which come in may see the light. **34**The light of the body is the eye: therefore when *thine eye* is single, thy whole body also is full of light; but when thine eye is evil, thy body also *is* full of darkness. **35**Take heed therefore that the light which is in thee be not darkness. **36**If thy whole body therefore *be* full of light, having no part dark, the whole shall be full of light, as when the bright shining of a candle doth give thee light.

The scribes and Pharisees reproved by Jesus

Matthew 23.1–36

37And as he spake, a certain Pharisee besought him to dine with him: and he went in, and sat down to meat. **38**And when the Pharisee saw *it*, he marvelled that he had not first washed before dinner. **39**And the Lord said unto him, Now do ye Pharisees make clean the outside of the cup and the platter; but your inward part is full of ravening and wickedness. **40**Ye fools, did not he that made that which is without make that which is within also?

41But rather give alms of such things as ye have; and, behold, all things are clean unto you.

42But woe unto you, Pharisees! for ye tithe mint and rue and all manner of herbs, and pass over judgment and the love of God: these ought ye to have done, and not to leave the other undone. **43**Woe unto you, Pharisees! for ye love the uppermost seats in the synagogues, and greetings in the markets. **44**Woe unto you, scribes and Pharisees, hypocrites! for ye are as graves which appear not, and the men that walk over *them* are not aware *of them*.

45Then answered one of the lawyers, and said unto him, Master, thus saying thou reproachest us also. **46**And he said, Woe unto you also, *ye* lawyers! for ye lade men with burdens grievous to be borne, and ye yourselves touch not the burdens with one of your fingers.

47Woe unto you! for ye build the sepulchres of the prophets, and your fathers killed them. **48**Truly ye bear witness that ye allow the deeds of your fathers: for they indeed killed them, and ye build their sepulchres. **49**Therefore also said the wisdom of God, I will send them prophets and apostles, and *some* of them they shall slay and persecute: [50]that the blood of all the prophets, which was shed from the foundation of the world, may be required of this generation; [51]from the blood of Abel unto the blood of Zacharias, which perished between the altar and the temple: verily I say unto you, It shall be required of this generation.

[52]Woe unto you, lawyers! for ye have taken away the key of knowledge: ye entered not in yourselves, and them that were entering in ye hindered.

[53]And as he said these things unto them, the scribes and the Pharisees began to urge *him* vehemently, and to provoke him to speak of many things: [54]laying wait for him, and seeking to catch something out of his mouth, that they might accuse him.

12 In the mean time, when there were gathered together an innumerable multitude of people, insomuch that they trode one upon another, he began to say unto his disciples first of all, Beware ye of the leaven of the Pharisees, which is hypocrisy. [2]For there is nothing covered, that shall not be revealed; neither hid, that shall not be known. [3]Therefore whatsoever ye have spoken in darkness shall be heard in the light; and that which ye have spoken in the ear in closets shall be proclaimed upon the housetops.

[4]And I say unto you my friends, Be not afraid of them that kill the body, and after that have no more that they can do. [5]But I will forewarn you whom ye shall fear: Fear him, which after he hath killed hath power to cast into hell; yea, I say unto you, Fear him. [6]Are not five sparrows sold for two farthings, and not one of them is forgotten before God? [7]But even the very hairs of your head are all numbered. Fear not therefore: ye are of more value than many sparrows.

[8]Also I say unto you, Whosoever shall confess me before men, him shall the Son of man also confess before the angels of God: [9]but he that denieth me before men shall be denied before the angels of God.

[10]And whosoever shall speak a word against the Son of man, it shall be forgiven him: but unto him that blasphemeth against the Holy Ghost it shall not be forgiven.

11And when they bring you unto the synagogues, and *unto* magistrates, and powers, take ye no thought how or what thing ye shall answer, or what ye shall say: 12for the Holy Ghost shall teach you in the same hour what ye ought to say.

Warnings. Parable of the rich fool

Matthew 10.26–33

13And one of the company said unto him, Master, speak to my brother, that he divide the inheritance with me. 14And he said unto him, Man, who made me a judge or a divider over you? 15And he said unto them, Take heed, and beware of covetousness: for a man's life consisteth not in the abundance of the things which he possesseth.

16And he spake a parable unto them, saying, The ground of a certain rich man brought forth plentifully: 17and he thought within himself, saying, What shall I do, because I have no room where to bestow my fruits? 18And he said, This will I do: I will pull down my barns, and build greater; and there will I bestow all my fruits and my goods. 19And I will say to my soul, Soul, thou hast much goods laid up for many years; take thine ease, eat, drink, *and* be merry. 20But God said unto him, *Thou fool*, this night thy soul shall be required of thee: then whose shall those things be, which thou hast provided? 21So *is* he that layeth up treasure for himself, and is not rich toward God.

'Seek ye first the kingdom of God'

Matthew 6.25–34

22And he said unto his disciples, Therefore I say unto you, Take no thought for your life, what ye shall eat; neither for the body, what ye shall put on. 23The life is more than meat, and the body *is more* than raiment. 24Consider the ravens: for they neither sow nor reap; which neither have storehouse nor barn; and God feedeth them: how much more are ye better than the fowls? 25And which of you with taking thought can add to his stature one cubit? 26If ye then be not able to do that thing which is least, why take ye thought for the rest? 27Consider the lilies how they grow: they toil not, they spin not; and yet I say unto you, that Solomon in all his glory was not arrayed like one of these. 28If then God so clothe the grass, which is to day in the field, and to morrow is cast into the oven; how much more *will he clothe* you, O ye of little faith? ²⁹And seek not ye what ye shall eat, or what ye shall drink, neither be ye of doubtful mind. ³⁰For all these things do the nations of the world seek after: and your Father knoweth that ye have need of these things. ³¹But rather seek ye the kingdom of God; and all these things shall be added unto you.

³²Fear not, little flock; for it is your Father's good pleasure to give you the kingdom. ³³Sell that ye have, and give alms; provide yourselves bags which wax not old, a treasure in the heavens that faileth not, where no thief approacheth, neither moth corrupteth. ³⁴For where your treasure is, there will your heart be also.

³⁵Let your loins be girded about, and *your* lights burning; ³⁶and ye yourselves like unto men that wait for their lord, when he will return from the wedding; that when he cometh and knocketh, they may open unto him immediately. ³⁷Blessed *are* those servants, whom the lord when he cometh shall find watching: verily I say unto you, that he shall gird himself, and make them to sit down to meat,

and will come forth and serve them. ³⁸And if he shall come in the second watch, or come in the third watch, and find *them* so, blessed are those servants. ³⁹And this know, that if the goodman of the house had known what hour the thief would come, he would have watched, and not have suffered his house to be broken through. ⁴⁰Be ye therefore ready also: for the Son of man cometh at an hour when ye think not.

⁴¹Then Peter said unto him, Lord, speakest thou this parable unto us, or even to all? ⁴²And the Lord said, Who then is that faithful and wise steward, whom *his* lord shall make ruler over his household, to give *them their* portion of meat in due season? ⁴³Blessed *is* that servant, whom his lord when he cometh shall find so doing. ⁴⁴Of a truth I say unto you, that he will make him ruler over all that he hath. ⁴⁵But and if that servant say in his heart, My lord delayeth his coming; and shall begin to beat the menservants and maidens, and to eat and drink, and to be drunken; ⁴⁶the lord of that servant will come in a day when he looketh not for *him*, and at an hour when he is not aware, and will cut him in sunder, and will appoint him his portion with the unbelievers. ⁴⁷And that servant,

which knew his lord's will, and prepared not *himself*, neither did according to his will, shall be beaten with many *stripes*. ⁴⁸But he that knew not, and did commit things worthy of stripes, shall be beaten with few *stripes*. For unto whomsoever much is given, of him shall be much required: and to whom men have committed much, of him they will ask the more.

⁴⁹I am come to send fire on the earth; and what will I, if it be already kindled? ⁵⁰But I have a baptism to be baptized with; and how am I straitened till it be accomplished! ⁵¹Suppose ye that I am come to give peace on earth? I tell you, Nay; but rather division: ⁵²for from henceforth there shall be five in one house divided, three against two, and two against three. ⁵³The father shall be divided against the son, and the son against the father; the mother against the daughter, and the daughter against the mother; the mother in law against her daughter in law, and the daughter in law against her mother in law.

⁵⁴And he said also to the people, When ye see a cloud rise out of the west, straightway ye say, There cometh a shower; and so it is. ⁵⁵And when *ye see* the south wind blow, ye say, There will be heat; and it cometh to pass. ⁵⁶*Ye* hypocrites, ye can discern the face of the sky and of the earth; but how is it that ye do not discern this time? ⁵⁷Yea, and why even of yourselves judge ye not what is right?

⁵⁸When thou goest with thine adversary to the magistrate, *as thou art* in the way, give diligence that thou mayest be delivered from him; lest he hale thee to the judge, and the judge deliver thee to the officer, and the officer cast thee into prison. ⁵⁹I tell thee, thou shalt not depart thence, till thou hast paid the very last mite.

13 There were present at that season some that told him of the Galilaeans, whose blood Pilate had mingled with their sacrifices. ²And Jesus answering said unto them, Suppose ye that these Galilaeans were sinners above all the Galilaeans, because they suffered such things? ³I tell you, Nay: but, except ye repent, ye shall all likewise perish. ⁴Or those eighteen, upon whom the tower in Siloam fell, and slew them, think ye that they were sinners above all men that dwelt in Jerusalem? ⁵I tell you, Nay: but, except ye repent, ye shall all likewise perish.

6He spake also this parable; A certain *man* had a fig tree planted in his vineyard; and he came and sought fruit thereon, and found none. **7**Then said he unto the dresser of his vineyard, Behold, these three years I come seeking fruit on this fig tree, and find none: cut it down; why cumbereth it the ground? **8**And he answering said unto him, Lord, let it alone this year also, till I shall dig about it, and dung *it*: **9**and if it bear fruit, *well*: and if not, *then* after that thou shalt cut it down.

A woman healed on the sabbath

10And he was teaching in one of the synagogues on the sabbath. **11**And, behold, there was a woman which had a spirit of infirmity eighteen years, and was bowed together, and could in no wise lift up *herself*. **12**And when Jesus saw her, he called *her to him*, and said unto her, Woman, thou art loosed from thine infirmity. **13**And he laid *his* hands on her: and immediately she was made straight, and glorified God. **14**And the ruler of the synagogue answered with indignation, because that Jesus had healed on the sabbath day, and said unto the people, There are six days in which men ought to work: in them therefore come and be healed, and not on the sabbath day.

15The Lord then answered him, and said, *Thou* hypocrite, doth not each one of you on the sabbath loose his ox or *his* ass from the stall, and lead *him* away to watering? **16**And ought not this woman, being a daughter of Abraham, whom Satan hath bound, lo, these eighteen years, be loosed from this bond on the sabbath day? **17**And when he had said these things, all his adversaries were ashamed: and all the people rejoiced for all the glorious things that were done by him.

Parables of the kingdom of God

Matthew 13.31–33; Mark 4.30–32

18Then said he, Unto what is the kingdom of God like? and whereunto shall I resemble it? **19**It is like a grain of mustard seed, which a man took, and cast into his garden; and it grew, and waxed a great tree; and the fowls of the air lodged in the branches of it. **20**And again he said, Whereunto shall I liken the kingdom of God? ²¹It is like leaven, which a woman took and hid in three measures of meal, till the whole was leavened.

²²And he went through the cities and villages, teaching, and journeying toward Jerusalem. ²³Then said one unto him, Lord, are there few that be saved? And he said unto them, ²⁴Strive to enter in at the strait gate: for many, I say unto you, will seek to enter in, and shall not be able. ²⁵When once the master of the house is risen up, and hath shut to the door, and ye begin to stand without, and to knock at the door, saying, Lord, Lord, open unto us; and he shall answer and say unto you, I know you not whence ye are: ²⁶then shall ye begin to say, We have eaten and drunk in thy presence, and thou hast taught in our streets. ²⁷But he shall say, I tell you, I know you not whence ye are; depart from me, all *ye* workers of iniquity. ²⁸There shall be weeping and gnashing of teeth, when ye shall see Abraham, and Isaac, and Jacob, and all the prophets, in the kingdom of God, and you *yourselves* thrust out. ²⁹And they shall come from the east, and *from* the west, and from the north, and *from* the south, and shall sit down in the kingdom of God. ³⁰And, behold, there are last

which shall be first, and there are first which shall be last.

³¹The same day there came certain of the Pharisees, saying unto him, Get thee out, and depart hence: for Herod will kill thee. ³²And he said unto them, Go ye, and tell that fox, Behold, I cast out devils, and I do cures to day and to morrow, and the third *day* I shall be perfected. ³³Nevertheless I must walk to day, and to morrow, and the *day* following: for it cannot be that a prophet perish out of Jerusalem. ³⁴O Jerusalem, Jerusalem, which killest the prophets, and stonest them that are sent unto thee; how often would I have gathered thy children together, as a hen *doth gather* her brood under *her* wings, and ye would not! ³⁵Behold, your house is left unto you desolate: and verily I say unto you, Ye shall not see me, until *the time* come when ye shall say, Blessed *is* he that cometh in the name of the Lord.

Healing on the sabbath

14 And it came to pass, as he went into the house of one of the chief Pharisees to eat bread on the sabbath day, that they watched him. ²And, behold, there was a certain man before him which had the dropsy. ³And Jesus answering spake unto the lawyers and Pharisees, saying, Is it lawful to heal on the sabbath day? ⁴And they held their peace. And he took *him*, and healed him, and let him go; ⁵and answered them, saying, Which of you shall have an ass or an ox fallen into a pit, and will not straightway pull him out on the sabbath day? ⁶And they could not answer him again to these things.

⁷And he put forth a parable to those which were bidden, when he marked how they chose out the chief rooms; saying unto them, ⁸When thou art bidden of any *man* to a wedding, sit not down in the highest room; lest a more honourable man than thou be bidden of him; ⁹and he that bade thee and him come and say to thee, Give this man place; and thou begin with shame to take the lowest room. ¹⁰But when thou art bidden, go and sit down in the lowest room; that when he that bade thee cometh, he may say unto thee, Friend, go up higher: then shalt thou have worship in the presence of them that sit at meat with thee. ¹¹For whosoever exalteth himself shall be abased; and he that humbleth himself shall be exalted.

¹²Then said he also to him that bade him, When thou makest a dinner or a supper, call not thy friends, nor thy brethren, neither thy kinsmen, nor *thy* rich neighbours; lest they also bid thee again, and a recompence be made thee. ¹³But when thou makest a feast, call the poor, the maimed, the lame, the blind: ¹⁴and thou shalt be blessed; for they cannot recompense thee: for thou shalt be recompensed at the resurrection of the just.

Parable of the great supper
Matthew 22.1–10

¹⁵And when one of them that sat at meat with him heard these things, he said unto him, Blessed *is* he that shall eat bread in the kingdom of God. ¹⁶Then said he unto him, A certain man made a great supper, and bade many: ¹⁷and sent his servant at supper time to say to them that were bidden, Come; for all things are now ready. ¹⁸And they all with one *consent* began to make excuse. The first said unto him, I have bought a piece of ground, and I must needs go and see it: I pray thee have me excused. ¹⁹And another said, I have bought five yoke of oxen, and I go to prove them: I pray thee

have me excused. ²⁰And another said, I have married a wife, and therefore I cannot come. ²¹So that servant came, and shewed his lord these things. Then the master of the house being angry said to his servant, Go out quickly into the streets and lanes of the city, and bring in hither the poor, and the maimed, and the halt, and the blind. ²²And the servant said, Lord, it is done as thou hast commanded, and yet there is room. ²³And the lord said unto the servant, Go out into the highways and hedges, and compel *them* to come in, that my house may be filled. ²⁴For I say unto you, That none of those men which were bidden shall taste of my supper.

²⁵And there went great multitudes with him: and he turned, and said unto them, ²⁶If any *man* come to me, and hate not his father, and mother, and wife, and children, and brethren, and sisters, yea, and his own life also, he cannot be my disciple. ²⁷And whosoever doth not bear his cross, and come after me, cannot be my disciple.

²⁸For which of you, intending to build a tower, sitteth not down first, and counteth the cost, whether he have *sufficient* to finish *it*? ²⁹Lest haply, after he

hath laid the foundation, and is not able to finish *it*, all that behold *it* begin to mock him, ³⁰saying, This man began to build, and was not able to finish.

³¹Or what king, going to make war against another king, sitteth not down first, and consulteth whether he be able with ten thousand to meet him that cometh against him with twenty thousand? ³²Or else, while the other is yet a great way off, he sendeth an ambassage, and desireth conditions of peace.

³³So likewise, whosoever he be of you that forsaketh not all that he hath, he cannot be my disciple. ³⁴Salt *is* good: but if the salt have lost his savour, wherewith shall it be seasoned? ³⁵It is neither fit for the land, nor yet for the dunghill; *but* men cast it out. He that hath ears to hear, let him hear.

Parables: the lost sheep, the lost coin and the prodigal son

15 Then drew near unto him all the publicans and sinners for to hear him. ²And the Pharisees and scribes murmured, saying, This man receiveth sinners, and eateth with them.

³And he spake this parable unto them, saying, ⁴What man of you, having an hundred sheep, if he lose one of them, doth not leave the ninety and nine in the wilderness, and go after that which is lost, until he find it? ⁵And when he hath found *it*, he layeth *it* on his shoulders, rejoicing. ⁶And when he cometh home, he calleth together *his* friends and neighbours, saying unto them, Rejoice with me; for I have found my sheep which was lost. ⁷I say unto you, that likewise joy shall be in heaven over one sinner that repenteth, more than over ninety and nine just persons, which need no repentance.

⁸Either what woman having ten pieces of silver, if she lose one piece, doth not light a candle, and sweep the house, and seek diligently till she find *it*? ⁹And when she hath found *it*, she calleth *her* friends and *her* neighbours together, saying, Rejoice with me; for I have found the piece which I had lost. ¹⁰Likewise, I say unto you, there is joy in the presence of the angels of God over one sinner that repenteth.

¹¹And he said, A certain man had two sons: ¹²and the younger of them said to *his* father, Father, give me the portion of goods that falleth *to me*. And he divided unto them *his* living. ¹³And not many days after the younger son gathered all together, and took his journey into a far country, and there wasted his substance with riotous living. ¹⁴And when he had spent all, there arose a mighty famine in that land; and he began to be in want. ¹⁵And he went and joined himself to a citizen of that country; and he sent him into his fields to feed swine. ¹⁶And he would fain have filled his belly with the husks that the swine did eat: and no man gave unto him.

¹⁷And when he came to himself, he said, How many hired servants of my father's have bread enough and to spare, and I perish with hunger! ¹⁸I will arise and go to my father, and will say unto him, Father, I have sinned against heaven, and before thee, ¹⁹and am no more worthy to be called thy son: make me as one of thy hired servants.

²⁰And he arose, and came to his father. But when he was yet a great way off, his father saw him, and had compassion, and ran, and fell on his neck, and kissed him. ²¹And the son said unto him, Father, I have sinned against heaven, and in thy sight, and am

no more worthy to be called thy son. ²²But the father said to his servants, Bring forth the best robe, and put *it* on him; and put a ring on his hand, and shoes on *his* feet: ²³and bring hither the fatted calf, and kill *it*; and let us eat, and be merry: ²⁴for this my son was dead, and is alive again; he was lost, and is found. And they began to be merry.

²⁵Now his elder son was in the field: and as he came and drew nigh to the house, he heard musick and dancing. ²⁶And he called one of the servants, and asked what these things meant. ²⁷And he said unto him, Thy brother is come; and thy father hath killed the fatted calf, because he hath received him safe and sound. ²⁸And he was angry, and would not go in: therefore came his father out, and intreated him. ²⁹And he answering said to *his* father, Lo, these many years do I serve thee, neither transgressed I at any time thy commandment: and yet thou never gavest me a kid, that I might make merry with my friends: ³⁰but as soon as this thy son was come, which hath devoured thy living with harlots, thou hast killed for him the fatted calf.

³¹And he said unto him, Son, thou art ever with me, and all that I have is thine. ³²It was meet that we should make merry, and be glad: for this thy brother was dead, and is alive again; and was lost, and is found.

Parable of the unjust steward

16 And he said also unto his disciples, There was a certain rich man, which had a steward; and the same was accused unto him that he had wasted his goods. ²And he called him, and said unto him, How is it that I hear this of thee? give an account of thy stewardship; for thou mayest be no longer steward. ³Then the steward said within himself, What shall I do? for my lord taketh away from me the stewardship: I cannot dig; to beg I am ashamed. ⁴I am resolved what to do, that, when I am put out of the stewardship, they may receive me into their houses. ⁵So he called every one of his lord's debtors *unto him*, and said unto the first, How much owest thou unto my lord? ⁶And he said, An hundred measures of oil. And he said unto him, Take thy bill, and sit down quickly, and write fifty. ⁷Then said he to another, And how much owest thou? And he said, An hundred measures of wheat.

And he said unto him, Take thy bill, and write fourscore. 8And the lord commended the unjust steward, because he had done wisely: for the children of this world are in their generation wiser than the children of light.

9And I say unto you, Make to yourselves friends of the mammon of unrighteousness; that, when ye fail, they may receive you into everlasting habitations. 10He that is faithful in that which is least is faithful also in much: and he that is unjust in the least is unjust also in much. 11If therefore ye have not been faithful in the unrighteous mammon, who will commit to your trust the true *riches*? 12And if ye have not been faithful in that which is another man's, who shall give you that which is your own?

13No servant can serve two masters: for either he will hate the one, and love the other; or else he will hold to the one, and despise the other. Ye cannot serve God and mammon. 14And the Pharisees also, who were covetous, heard all these things: and they derided him. 15And he said unto them, Ye are they which justify yourselves before men; but God knoweth your hearts: for that which is highly esteemed among men is abomination in the sight of God.

16The law and the prophets *were* until John: since that time the kingdom of God is preached, and every man presseth into it. 17And it is easier for heaven and earth to pass, than one tittle of the law to fail. 18Whosoever putteth away his wife, and marrieth another, committeth adultery: and whosoever marrieth her that is put away from *her* husband committeth adultery.

The rich man and Lazarus

19There was a certain rich man, which was clothed in purple and fine linen, and fared sumptuously every day: 20and there was a certain beggar named Lazarus, which was laid at his gate, full of sores, 21and desiring to be fed with the crumbs which fell from the rich man's table: moreover the dogs came and licked his sores. 22And it came to pass, that the beggar died, and was carried by the angels into Abraham's bosom: the rich man also died, and was buried; 23and in hell he lift up his eyes, being in torments, and seeth Abraham afar off, and Lazarus in his bosom. 24And he cried and said, Father Abraham, have mercy on me, and send Lazarus, that he may dip the tip of his finger in water, and cool my tongue; for I am tormented in this flame.

²⁵But Abraham said, Son, remember that thou in thy lifetime receivedst thy good things, and likewise Lazarus evil things: but now he is comforted, and thou art tormented. ²⁶And beside all this, between us and you there is a great gulf fixed: so that they which would pass from hence to you cannot; neither can they pass to us, that *would come* from thence. ²⁷Then he said, I pray thee therefore, father, that thou wouldest send him to my father's house: ²⁸for I have five brethren; that he may testify unto them, lest they also come into this place of torment. ²⁹Abraham saith unto him, They have Moses and the prophets; let them hear them. ³⁰And he said, Nay, father Abraham: but if one went unto them from the dead, they will repent. ³¹And he said unto him, If they hear not Moses and the prophets, neither will they be persuaded, though one rose from the dead.

17 Then said he unto the disciples, It is impossible but that offences will come: but woe *unto him,* through whom they come! ²It were better for him that a millstone were hanged about his neck, and he cast into the sea, than that he should offend one of these little ones.

³Take heed to yourselves: If thy brother trespass against thee, rebuke him; and if he repent, forgive him. ⁴And if he trespass against thee seven times in a day, and seven times in a day turn again to thee, saying, I repent; thou shalt forgive him.

⁵And the apostles said unto the Lord, Increase our faith. ⁶And the Lord said, If ye had faith as a grain of mustard seed, ye might say unto this sycamine tree, Be thou plucked up by the root, and be thou planted in the sea; and it should obey you. ⁷But which of you, having a servant plowing or feeding cattle, will say unto him by and by, when he is come from the field, Go and sit down to meat? ⁸And will not rather say unto him, Make ready wherewith I may sup, and gird thyself, and serve me, till I have eaten and drunken; and afterward thou shalt eat and drink? ⁹Doth he thank that servant because he did the things that were commanded him? I trow not. ¹⁰So likewise ye, when ye shall have done all those things which are commanded you, say, We are unprofitable servants: we have done that which was our duty to do.

Healing of ten lepers

11And it came to pass, as he went to Jerusalem, that he passed through the midst of Samaria and Galilee. **12**And as he entered into a certain village, there met him ten men that were lepers, which stood afar off: **13**and they lifted up *their* voices, and said, Jesus, Master, have mercy on us. **14**And when he saw *them*, he said unto them, Go shew yourselves unto the priests. And it came to pass, that, as they went, they were cleansed. **15**And one of them, when he saw that he was healed, turned back, and with a loud voice glorified God, **16**and fell down on *his* face at his feet, giving him thanks: and he was a Samaritan. **17**And Jesus answering said, Were there not ten cleansed? but where *are* the nine? **18**There are not found that returned to give glory to God, save this stranger. **19**And he said unto him, Arise, go thy way: thy faith hath made thee whole.

The coming of the Son of man

Matthew 24; Mark 13

20And when he was demanded of the Pharisees, when the kingdom of God should come, he answered them and said, The kingdom of God cometh not with observation: **21**neither shall they say, Lo here! or, lo there! for, behold, the kingdom of God is within you.

22And he said unto the disciples, The days will come, when ye shall desire to see one of the days of the Son of man, and ye shall not see *it*. **23**And they shall say to you, See here; or, see there: go not after *them*, nor follow *them*. **24**For as the lightning, that lighteneth out of the one *part* under heaven, shineth unto the other *part* under heaven; so shall also the Son of man be in his day. **25**But first must he suffer many things, and be rejected of this generation.

26And as it was in the days of Noe, so shall it be also in the days of the Son of man. **27**They did eat, they drank, they married wives, they were given in marriage, until the day that Noe entered into the ark, and the flood came, and destroyed them all. **28**Likewise also as it was in the days of Lot; they did eat, they drank, they bought, they sold, they planted, they builded; **29**but the same day that Lot went out of Sodom it rained fire and brimstone from heaven, and destroyed *them* all. **30**Even thus shall it be in the day when the

Son of man is revealed.

31 In that day, he which shall be upon the housetop, and his stuff in the house, let him not come down to take it away: and he that is in the field, let him likewise not return back. ³²Remember Lot's wife. ³³Whosoever shall seek to save his life shall lose it; and whosoever shall lose his life shall preserve it. ³⁴I tell you, in that night there shall be two *men* in one bed; the one shall be taken, and the other shall be left. ³⁵Two *women* shall be grinding together; the one shall be taken, and the other left. ³⁶Two *men* shall be in the field; the one shall be taken, and the other left.

³⁷And they answered and said unto him, Where, Lord? And he said unto them, Wheresoever the body *is*, thither will the eagles be gathered together.

Parables on prayer

18 And he spake a parable unto them *to this end*, that men ought always to pray, and not to faint; ²saying, There was in a city a judge, which feared not God, neither regarded man: ³and there was a widow in that city; and she came unto him, saying, Avenge me of mine adversary. ⁴And he would not for a while: but afterward he said within himself, Though I fear not God, nor regard man; ⁵yet because this widow troubleth me, I will avenge her, lest by her continual coming she weary me.

6And the Lord said, Hear what the unjust judge saith. ⁷And shall not God avenge his own elect, which cry day and night unto him, though he bear long with them? ⁸I tell you that he will avenge them speedily. Nevertheless when the Son of man cometh, shall he find faith on the earth?

9And he spake this parable unto certain which trusted in themselves that they were righteous, and despised others: ¹⁰Two men went up into the temple to pray; the one a Pharisee, and the other a publican. ¹¹The Pharisee stood and prayed thus with himself, God, I thank thee, that I am not as other men *are*, extortioners, unjust, adulterers, or even as this publican. ¹²I fast twice in the week, I give tithes of all that I possess. ¹³And the publican, standing afar off, would not lift up so much as *his* eyes unto heaven, but smote upon his breast, saying, God be merciful to me a sinner. ¹⁴I tell you, this man went down to his house justified *rather* than the other: for every one that exalteth himself shall be abased; and he that humbleth himself shall be exalted.

¹⁵And they brought unto him also infants, that he would touch them: but when *his* disciples saw *it*, they rebuked them. ¹⁶But Jesus called them *unto him*, and said, Suffer little children to come unto me, and forbid them not: for of such is the kingdom of God. ¹⁷Verily I say unto you, Whosoever shall not receive the kingdom of God as a little child shall in no wise enter therein.

'What shall I do to inherit eternal life?'

Matthew 19.16–26; Mark 10.17–27

¹⁸And a certain ruler asked him, saying, Good Master, what shall I do to inherit eternal life? ¹⁹And Jesus said unto him, Why callest thou me good? none *is* good, save one, *that is*, God. ²⁰Thou knowest the commandments, Do not commit adultery, Do not kill, Do not steal, Do not bear false witness, Honour thy father and thy mother. ²¹And he said, All these have I kept from my youth up. ²²Now when Jesus heard these things, he said unto him, Yet lackest thou one thing: sell all that thou hast, and distribute unto the poor, and thou shalt have treasure in heaven: and come, follow me.

²³And when he heard this, he was very sorrowful: for he was very rich. ²⁴And when Jesus saw that he was very sorrowful, he said, How hardly shall they that have riches enter into the kingdom of God! ²⁵For it is easier for a camel to go through a needle's eye, than for a rich man to enter into the kingdom of God. ²⁶And they that heard *it* said, Who then can be saved? ²⁷And he said, The things which are impossible with men are possible with God.

²⁸Then Peter said, Lo, we have left all, and followed thee. ²⁹And he said unto them, Verily I say unto you, There is no man that hath left house, or parents, or brethren, or wife, or children, for the kingdom of God's sake, ³⁰who shall not receive manifold more in this present time, and in the world to come life everlasting.

Jesus foretells His sufferings, death and resurrection

Matthew 20.17–19; Mark 10.32–34

³¹Then he took *unto him* the twelve, and said unto them,

Behold, we go up to Jerusalem, and all things that are written by the prophets concerning the Son of man shall be accomplished. 32For he shall be delivered unto the Gentiles, and shall be mocked, and spitefully entreated, and spitted on: 33and they shall scourge *him*, and put him to death: and the third day he shall rise again. 34And they understood none of these things: and this saying was hid from them, neither knew they the things which were spoken.

A blind man cured at Jericho

Matthew 20.29–34; Mark 10.46–52

35And it came to pass, that as he was come nigh unto Jericho, a certain blind man sat by the way side begging: 36and hearing the multitude pass by, he asked what it meant. 37And they told him, that Jesus of Nazareth passeth by. 38And he cried, saying, Jesus, *thou* Son of David, have mercy on me. 39And they which went before rebuked him, that he should hold his peace: but he cried so much the more, *Thou* Son of David, have mercy on me.

40And Jesus stood, and commanded him to be brought unto him: and when he was come near, he asked him, 41saying, What wilt thou that I shall do unto thee? And he said, Lord, that I may receive my sight. 42And Jesus said unto him, Receive thy sight: thy faith hath saved thee. 43And immediately he received his sight, and followed him, glorifying God: and all the people, when they saw *it*, gave praise unto God.

19 And *Jesus* entered and passed through Jericho. 2And, behold, *there was* a man named Zacchaeus, which was the chief among the publicans, and he was rich. 3And he sought to see Jesus who he was; and could not for the press, because he was little of stature. 4And he ran before, and climbed up into a sycomore tree to see him: for he was to pass that *way*. 5And when Jesus came to the place, he looked up, and saw him, and said unto him, Zacchaeus, make haste, and come down; for to day I must abide at thy house. 6And he made haste, and came down, and received him joyfully.

7And when they saw *it*, they all murmured, saying, That he was gone to be guest with a man that is a sinner. 8And Zacchaeus stood, and said unto the Lord; Behold, Lord, the half of my goods I give to the poor; and if I have taken any thing from any man by false accusation, I restore *him* fourfold. 9And Jesus said unto him, This day is salvation come to this house, forsomuch as he also is a son of Abraham. 10For the Son of man is come to seek and to save that which was lost.

Parable of the pounds

11And as they heard these things, he added and spake a parable, because he was nigh to Jerusalem, and because they thought that the kingdom of God should immediately appear. 12He said therefore, A certain nobleman went into a far country to receive for himself a kingdom, and to return. 13And he called his ten servants, and delivered them ten pounds, and said unto them, Occupy till I come. 14But his citizens hated him, and sent a message after him, saying, We will not have this *man* to reign over us. 15And it came to pass, that when he was returned, having received the kingdom, then he commanded these servants to be called unto him, to whom he had given the money, that he might know how much every man had gained by trading. 16Then came the first, saying, Lord, thy pound hath gained ten pounds. 17And he said unto him, Well, thou good servant: because thou hast been faithful in a very little, have thou authority over ten cities. 18And the second came, saying, Lord, thy pound hath gained five pounds. 19And he said likewise to him, Be thou also over five cities. 20And another came, saying, Lord, behold, *here* is thy pound, which I have kept laid up in a napkin: 21for I feared thee, because thou art an austere man: thou takest up that thou layedst not down, and reapest that thou didst not sow. 22And he saith unto him, Out of thine own mouth will I judge thee, *thou* wicked servant. Thou knewest that I was an austere man, taking up that I laid not down, and reaping that I did not sow: 23wherefore then gavest not thou my money into the bank, that at my coming I might have required mine own with usury? 24And he said unto them that stood by, Take from him the pound, and give *it* to him that hath ten pounds. 25(And they said unto him, Lord, he hath ten pounds.) 26For I say unto you, That unto every one which hath shall be given; and from him that hath not, even that he hath shall be taken away from him. 27But those mine enemies, which would not that I should reign over them, bring hither, and slay *them* before me.

The triumphal entry into Jerusalem. The temple cleansed

Matthew 21.1–16; Mark 11.1–18; John 12.12–16

28And when he had thus spoken, he went before, ascending up to Jerusalem. **29**And it came to pass, when he was come nigh to Bethphage and Bethany, at the mount called *the mount* of Olives, he sent two of his disciples, **30**saying, Go ye into the village over against *you*; in the which at your entering ye shall find a colt tied, whereon yet never man sat: loose him, and bring *him hither*. **31**And if any man ask you, Why do ye loose *him*? thus shall ye say unto him, Because the Lord hath need of him.

32And they that were sent went their way, and found even as he had said unto them. **33**And as they were loosing the colt, the owners thereof said unto them, Why loose ye the colt? **34**And they said, The Lord hath need of him. **35**And they brought him to Jesus: and they cast their garments upon the colt, and they set Jesus thereon. **36**And as he went, they spread their clothes in the way.

37And when he was come nigh, even now at the descent of the mount of Olives, the whole multitude of the disciples began to rejoice and praise God with a loud voice for all the mighty works that they had seen; **38**saying, Blessed *be* the King that cometh in the name of the Lord: peace in heaven, and glory in the highest.

39And some of the Pharisees from among the multitude said unto him, Master, rebuke thy disciples. **40**And he answered and said unto them, I tell you that, if these should hold their peace, the stones would immediately cry out.

41And when he was come near, he beheld the city, and wept over it, **42**saying, If thou hadst known, even thou, at least in this thy day, the things *which belong* unto thy peace! but now they are hid from thine eyes. **43**For the days shall come upon thee, that thine enemies shall cast a trench about thee, and compass thee round, and keep thee in on every side, **44**and shall lay thee even with the ground, and thy children within thee; and they shall not leave in thee one stone upon another; because thou knewest not the time of thy visitation.

45And he went into the temple,

and began to cast out them that sold therein, and them that bought; ⁴⁶saying unto them, It is written, My house is the house of prayer: but ye have made it a den of thieves. ⁴⁷And he taught daily in the temple. But the chief priests and the scribes and the chief of the people sought to destroy him, ⁴⁸and could not find what they might do: for all the people were very attentive to hear him.

The authority of Jesus

Matthew 21.23–27; Mark 11.27–33

20 And it came to pass, *that* on one of those days, as he taught the people in the temple, and preached the gospel, the chief priests and the scribes came upon *him* with the elders, ²and spake unto him, saying, Tell us, by what authority doest thou these things? or who is he that gave thee this authority?

³And he answered and said unto them, I will also ask you one thing; and answer me: ⁴The baptism of John, was it from heaven, or of men? ⁵And they reasoned with themselves, saying, If we shall say, From heaven; he will say, Why then believed ye him not? ⁶But and if we say, Of men; all the people will stone us: for they be persuaded that John was a prophet. ⁷And they answered, that they could not tell whence *it was.* ⁸And Jesus said unto them, Neither tell I you by what authority I do these things.

Parable of the wicked husbandmen

Matthew 21.33–46; Mark 12.1–12

⁹Then began he to speak to the people this parable; A certain man planted a vineyard, and let it forth to husbandmen, and went into a far country for a long time. ¹⁰And at the season he sent a servant to the husbandmen, that they should give him of the fruit of the vineyard: but the husbandmen beat him, and sent *him* away empty. ¹¹And again he sent another servant: and they beat him also, and entreated *him* shamefully, and sent *him* away empty. ¹²And again he sent a third: and they wounded him also, and cast *him* out. ¹³Then said the lord of the vineyard, What shall I do? I will send my beloved son: it may be they will reverence *him* when they see him. ¹⁴But when the husbandmen saw him, they reasoned among themselves, saying, This is the heir: come, let us kill him, that

the inheritance may be ours. ¹⁵So they cast him out of the vineyard, and killed *him*. What therefore shall the lord of the vineyard do unto them? ¹⁶He shall come and destroy these husbandmen, and shall give the vineyard to others. And when they heard *it*, they said, God forbid.

¹⁷And he beheld them, and said, What is this then that is written, The stone which the builders rejected, the same is become the head of the corner? ¹⁸Whosoever shall fall upon that stone shall be broken; but on whomsoever it shall fall, it will grind him to powder.

Jesus silences His enemies

Matthew 22.15–45; Mark 12.13–40

¹⁹And the chief priests and the scribes the same hour sought to lay hands on him; and they feared the people: for they perceived that he had spoken this parable against them.

²⁰And they watched *him*, and sent forth spies, which should feign themselves just men, that they might take hold of his words, that so they might deliver him unto the power and authority of the governor. ²¹And they asked him, saying, Master, we know that thou sayest and teachest rightly, neither acceptest thou the person *of any*, but teachest the way of God truly: ²²is it lawful for us to give tribute unto Caesar, or no? ²³But he perceived their craftiness, and said unto them, Why tempt ye me? ²⁴Shew me a penny. Whose image and superscription hath it? They answered and said, Caesar's. ²⁵And he said unto them, Render therefore unto Caesar the things which be Caesar's, and unto God the things which be God's. ²⁶And they could not take hold of his words before the people: and they marvelled at his answer, and held their peace.

²⁷Then came to *him* certain of the Sadducees, which deny that there is any resurrection; and they asked him, ²⁸saying, Master, Moses wrote unto us, If any man's brother die, having a wife, and he die without children, that his brother should take his wife, and raise up seed unto his brother. ²⁹There were therefore seven brethren: and the first took a wife, and died without children. ³⁰And the second took her to wife, and he died childless. ³¹And the third took her; and in like manner the seven also: and

they left no children, and died. [32]Last of all the woman died also. [33]Therefore in the resurrection whose wife of them is she? for seven had her to wife.

[34]And Jesus answering said unto them, The children of this world marry, and are given in marriage: [35]but they which shall be accounted worthy to obtain that world, and the resurrection from the dead, neither marry, nor are given in marriage: [36]neither can they die any more: for they are equal unto the angels; and are the children of God, being the children of the resurrection. [37]Now that the dead are raised, even Moses shewed at the bush, when he calleth the Lord the God of Abraham, and the God of Isaac, and the God of Jacob. [38]For he is not a God of the dead, but of the living: for all live unto him. [39]Then certain of the scribes answering said, Master, thou hast well said. [40]And after that they durst not ask him any *question at all.*

[41]And he said unto them, How say they that Christ is David's son? [42]And David himself saith in the book of Psalms, The Lord said unto my Lord, Sit thou on my right hand, [43]till I make thine enemies thy footstool. [44]David therefore calleth him Lord, how is he then his son?

[45]Then in the audience of all the people he said unto his disciples, [46]Beware of the scribes, which desire to walk in long robes, and love greetings in the markets, and the highest seats in the synagogues, and the chief rooms at feasts; [47]which devour widows' houses, and for a shew make long prayers: the same shall receive greater damnation.

The widow's mite
Mark 12.41–44

21 And he looked up, and saw the rich men casting their gifts into the treasury. [2]And he saw also a certain poor widow casting in thither two mites. [3]And he said, Of a truth I say unto you, that this poor widow hath cast in more than they all: [4]for all these have of their abundance cast in unto the offerings of God: but she of her penury hath cast in all the living that she had.

The destruction of the temple and the return of Christ foretold
Matthew 24.1–36; Mark 13.1–32

[5]And as some spake of the

temple, how it was adorned with goodly stones and gifts, he said, [6]*As for* these things which ye behold, the days will come, in the which there shall not be left one stone upon another, that shall not be thrown down. [7]And they asked him, saying, Master, but when shall these things be? and what sign *will there be* when these things shall come to pass?

[8]And he said, Take heed that ye be not deceived: for many shall come in my name, saying, I am *Christ*; and the time draweth near: go ye not therefore after them. [9]But when ye shall hear of wars and commotions, be not terrified: for these things must first come to pass; but the end *is* not by and by. [10]Then said he unto them, Nation shall rise against nation, and kingdom against kingdom: [11]and great earthquakes shall be in divers places, and famines, and pestilences; and fearful sights and great signs shall there be from heaven.

[12]But before all these, they shall lay their hands on *you*, and persecute *you*, delivering you up to the synagogues, and into prisons, being brought before kings and rulers for my name's sake. [13]And it shall turn to you for a testimony. [14]Settle *it* therefore in your hearts, not to meditate before what ye shall answer: [15]for I will give you a mouth and wisdom, which all your adversaries shall not be able to gainsay nor resist. [16]And ye shall be betrayed both by parents, and brethren, and kinsfolks, and friends; and *some* of you shall they cause to be put to death. [17]And ye shall be hated of all *men* for my name's sake. [18]But there shall not an hair of your head perish. [19]In your patience possess ye your souls.

[20]And when ye shall see Jerusalem compassed with armies, then know that the desolation thereof is nigh. [21]Then let them which are in Judaea flee to the mountains; and let them which are in the midst of it depart out; and let not them that are in the countries enter thereinto. [22]For these be the days of vengeance, that all things which are written may be fulfilled. [23]But woe unto them that are with child, and to them that give suck, in those days! for there shall be great distress in the land, and wrath upon this people. [24]And they shall fall by the edge of the sword, and shall be led away captive into all nations: and Jerusalem shall be trodden down of the Gentiles, until the times of the Gentiles be fulfilled.

25And there shall be signs in the sun, and in the moon, and in the stars; and upon the earth distress of nations, with perplexity; the sea and the waves roaring; 26men's hearts failing them for fear, and for looking after those things which are coming on the earth: for the powers of heaven shall be shaken. 27And then shall they see the Son of man coming in a cloud with power and great glory. 28And when these things begin to come to pass, then look up, and lift up your heads; for your redemption draweth nigh.

29And he spake to them a parable; Behold the fig tree, and all the trees; 30when they now shoot forth, ye see and know of your own selves that summer is now nigh at hand. 31So likewise ye, when ye see these things come to pass, know ye that the kingdom of God is nigh at hand. 32Verily I say unto you, This generation shall not pass away, till all be fulfilled. 33Heaven and earth shall pass away: but my words shall not pass away.

34And take heed to yourselves, lest at any time your hearts be overcharged with surfeiting, and drunkenness, and cares of this life, and *so* that day come upon you unawares.

35For as a snare shall it come on all them that dwell on the face of the whole earth. 36Watch ye therefore, and pray always, that ye may be accounted worthy to escape all these things that shall come to pass, and to stand before the Son of man.

37And in the day time he was teaching in the temple; and at night he went out, and abode in the mount that is called *the mount* of Olives. 38And all the people came early in the morning to him in the temple, for to hear him.

22 Now the feast of unleavened bread drew nigh, which is called the Passover. 2And the chief priests and scribes sought how they might kill him; for they feared the people.

3Then entered Satan into Judas surnamed Iscariot, being of the number of the twelve. 4And he went his way, and communed with the chief priests and captains, how he might betray him unto them. 5And they were glad, and covenanted to give him money. 6And he promised, and sought opportunity to betray him unto them in the absence of the multitude.

The last supper

Matthew 26.17–35; Mark 14.12–25

7Then came the day of unleavened bread, when the passover must be killed. **8**And he sent Peter and John, saying, Go and prepare us the passover, that we may eat. **9**And they said unto him, Where wilt thou that we prepare? **10**And he said unto them, Behold, when ye are entered into the city, there shall a man meet you, bearing a pitcher of water; follow him into the house where he entereth in. **11**And ye shall say unto the goodman of the house, The Master saith unto thee, Where is the guestchamber, where I shall eat the passover with my disciples? **12**And he shall shew you a large upper room furnished: there make ready. **13**And they went, and found as he had said unto them: and they made ready the passover.

14And when the hour was come, he sat down, and the twelve apostles with him. **15**And he said unto them, With desire I have desired to eat this passover with you before I suffer: **16**for I say unto you, I will not any more eat thereof, until it be fulfilled in the kingdom of God. **17**And he took the cup, and gave thanks, and said, Take this, and divide *it* among yourselves: **18**for I say unto you, I will not drink of the fruit of the vine, until the kingdom of God shall come.

19And he took bread, and gave thanks, and brake *it*, and gave unto them, saying, This is my body which is given for you: this do in remembrance of me. **20**Likewise also the cup after supper, saying, This cup *is* the new testament in my blood, which is shed for you. **21**But, behold, the hand of him that betrayeth me *is* with me on the table. **22**And truly the Son of man goeth, as it was determined: but woe unto that man by whom he is betrayed! **23**And they began to enquire among themselves, which of them it was that should do this thing.

24And there was also a strife among them, which of them should be accounted the greatest. **25**And he said unto them, The kings of the Gentiles exercise lordship over them; and they that exercise authority upon them are called benefactors. **26**But ye *shall* not *be* so: but he that is greatest among you, let him be as the younger; and he that is chief, as he that doth serve. **27**For whether *is* greater, he that sitteth at meat, or he that serveth? *is* not he that sitteth at meat? but I am among you as he that serveth. ²⁸Ye are they which have continued with me in my temptations. ²⁹And I appoint unto you a kingdom, as my Father hath appointed unto me; ³⁰that ye may eat and drink at my table in my kingdom, and sit on thrones judging the twelve tribes of Israel.

³¹And the Lord said, Simon, Simon, behold, Satan hath desired *to have* you, that he may sift *you* as wheat: ³²but I have prayed for thee, that thy faith fail not: and when thou art converted, strengthen thy brethren. ³³And he said unto him, Lord, I am ready to go with thee, both into prison, and to death. ³⁴And he said, I tell thee, Peter, the cock shall not crow this day, before that thou shalt thrice deny that thou knowest me.

³⁵And he said unto them, When I sent you without purse, and scrip, and shoes, lacked ye any thing? And they said, Nothing. ³⁶Then said he unto them, But now, he that hath a purse, let him take *it*, and likewise *his* scrip: and he that hath no sword, let him sell his garment, and buy one. ³⁷For I say unto you, that this that is written must yet be accomplished in me, And he was reckoned among the transgressors: for the things concerning me have an end.

³⁸And they said, Lord, behold, here *are* two swords. And he said unto them, It is enough.

Gethsemane. Arrest of Jesus

Matthew 26.36–56; Mark 14.32–52; John 18.1–12

³⁹ And he came out, and went, as he was wont, to the mount of Olives; and his disciples also followed him. ⁴⁰And when he was at the place, he said unto them, Pray that ye enter not into temptation.

⁴¹And he was withdrawn from them about a stone's cast, and kneeled down, and prayed, ⁴²saying, Father, if thou be willing, remove this cup from me: nevertheless not my will, but thine, be done. ⁴³And there appeared an angel unto him from heaven, strengthening him. ⁴⁴And being in an agony he prayed more earnestly: and his sweat was as it were great drops of blood falling down to the ground. ⁴⁵And when he rose up from prayer, and was come to his disciples, he found them sleeping for sorrow, ⁴⁶and said unto them, Why sleep ye? rise and pray, lest ye enter into temptation.

⁴⁷And while he yet spake,

behold a multitude, and he that was called Judas, one of the twelve, went before them, and drew near unto Jesus to kiss him. ⁴⁸But Jesus said unto him, Judas, betrayest thou the Son of man with a kiss?

⁴⁹When they which were about him saw what would follow, they said unto him, Lord, shall we smite with the sword? ⁵⁰And one of them smote the servant of the high priest, and cut off his right ear. ⁵¹And Jesus answered and said, Suffer ye thus far. And he touched his ear, and healed him.

⁵²Then Jesus said unto the chief priests, and captains of the temple, and the elders, which were come to him, Be ye come out, as against a thief, with swords and staves? ⁵³When I was daily with you in the temple, ye stretched forth no hands against me: but this is your hour, and the power of darkness.

Before the high priest. Peter's denial

Matthew 26.57–75; Mark 14.53–72; John 18.13–27

⁵⁴Then took they *him*, and led him, and brought him into the high priest's house. And Peter followed afar off.

⁵⁵And when they had kindled a fire in the midst of the hall, and were set down together, Peter sat down among them. ⁵⁶But a certain maid beheld him as he sat by the fire, and earnestly looked upon him, and said, This man was also with him. ⁵⁷And he denied him, saying, Woman, I know him not. ⁵⁸And after a little while another saw him, and said, Thou art also of them. And Peter said, Man, I am not. ⁵⁹And about the space of one hour after another confidently affirmed, saying, Of a truth this *fellow* also was with him: for he is a Galilaean. ⁶⁰And Peter said, Man, I know not what thou sayest. And immediately, while he yet spake, the cock crew. ⁶¹And the Lord turned, and looked upon Peter. And Peter remembered the word of the Lord, how he had said unto him, Before the cock crow, thou shalt deny me thrice. ⁶²And Peter went out, and wept bitterly.

⁶³And the men that held Jesus mocked him, and smote *him*. ⁶⁴And when they had blindfolded him, they struck him on the face, and asked him, saying, Prophesy, who is it that smote thee? ⁶⁵And many other things blasphemously spake they against him.

⁶⁶And as soon as it was day, the elders of the people and the chief

priests and the scribes came together, and led him into their council, saying, 67Art thou the Christ? tell us. And he said unto them, If I tell you, ye will not believe: 68and if I also ask *you*, ye will not answer me, nor let *me* go. 69Hereafter shall the Son of man sit on the right hand of the power of God. 70Then said they all, Art thou then the Son of God? And he said unto them, Ye say that I am. 71And they said, What need we any further witness? for we ourselves have heard of his own mouth.

Jesus before Pilate and Herod

Matthew 27.11–31; Mark 15.1–19; John 18.28–19.16

23 And the whole multitude of them arose, and led him unto Pilate.

2And they began to accuse him, saying, We found this *fellow* perverting the nation, and forbidding to give tribute to Caesar, saying that he himself is Christ a King. 3And Pilate asked him, saying, Art thou the King of the Jews? And he answered him and said, Thou sayest *it*.

4Then said Pilate to the chief priests and *to* the people, I find no fault in this man. 5And they were the more fierce, saying, He stirreth up the people, teaching throughout all Jewry, beginning from Galilee to this place.

6When Pilate heard of Galilee, he asked whether the man were a Galilaean. 7And as soon as he knew that he belonged unto Herod's jurisdiction, he sent him to Herod, who himself also was at Jerusalem at that time.

8And when Herod saw Jesus, he was exceeding glad: for he was desirous to see him of a long *season*, because he had heard many things of him; and he hoped to have seen some miracle done by him. 9Then he questioned with him in many words; but he answered him nothing. 10And the chief priests and scribes stood and vehemently accused him. 11And Herod with his men of war set him at nought, and mocked *him*, and arrayed him in a gorgeous robe, and sent him again to Pilate. 12And the same day Pilate and Herod were made friends together: for before they were at enmity between themselves.

13And Pilate, when he had called together the chief priests and the rulers and the people,

¹⁴said unto them, Ye have brought this man unto me, as one that perverteth the people: and, behold, I, having examined *him* before you, have found no fault in this man touching those things whereof ye accuse him: ¹⁵no, nor yet Herod: for I sent you to him; and, lo, nothing worthy of death is done unto him. ¹⁶I will therefore chastise him, and release *him*. ¹⁷(For of necessity he must release one unto them at the feast.) ¹⁸And they cried out all at once, saying, Away with this *man*, and release unto us Barabbas: ¹⁹(who for a certain sedition made in the city, and for murder, was cast into prison.)

The crucifixion, death and burial of Jesus

Matthew 27.32–66; Mark 15.20–47; John 19.16–42

²⁰Pilate therefore, willing to release Jesus, spake again to them. ²¹But they cried, saying, Crucify *him*, crucify him. ²²And he said unto them the third time, Why, what evil hath he done? I have found no cause of death in him: I will therefore chastise him, and let *him* go. ²³And they were instant with loud voices, requiring that he might be crucified. And the voices of them and of the chief priests prevailed. ²⁴And Pilate gave sentence that it should be as they required. ²⁵And he released unto them him that for sedition and murder was cast into prison, whom they had desired; but he delivered Jesus to their will.

²⁶And as they led him away, they laid hold upon one Simon, a Cyrenian, coming out of the country, and on him they laid the cross, that he might bear *it* after Jesus. ²⁷And there followed him a great company of people, and of women, which also bewailed and lamented him. ²⁸But Jesus turning unto them said, Daughters of Jerusalem, weep not for me, but weep for yourselves, and for your children. ²⁹For, behold, the days are coming, in the which they shall say, Blessed *are* the barren, and the wombs that never bare, and the paps which never gave suck. ³⁰Then shall they begin to say to the mountains, Fall on us; and to the hills, Cover us. ³¹For if they do these things in a green tree, what shall be done in the dry? ³²And there were also two other, malefactors, led with him to be put to death. ³³And when they were come to the place, which is called Calvary, there they crucified him, and the malefactors, one on the right hand, and the other on the left. ³⁴Then said Jesus, Father,

forgive them; for they know not what they do. And they parted his raiment, and cast lots.

35And the people stood beholding. And the rulers also with them derided *him*, saying, He saved others; let him save himself, if he be Christ, the chosen of God. 36And the soldiers also mocked him, coming to him, and offering him vinegar, 37and saying, If thou be the king of the Jews, save thyself. 38And a superscription also was written over him in letters of Greek, and Latin, and Hebrew, THIS IS THE KING OF THE JEWS.

39And one of the malefactors which were hanged railed on him, saying, If thou be Christ, save thyself and us. 40But the other answering rebuked him, saying, Dost not thou fear God, seeing thou art in the same condemnation? 41And we indeed justly; for we receive the due reward of our deeds: but this man hath done nothing amiss. 42And he said unto Jesus, Lord, remember me when thou comest into thy kingdom. 43And Jesus said unto him, Verily I say unto thee, To day shalt thou be with me in paradise.

44And it was about the sixth hour, and there was a darkness over all the earth until the ninth hour. 45And the sun was darkened, and the veil of the temple was rent in the midst. 46And when Jesus had cried with a loud voice, he said, Father, into thy hands I commend my spirit: and having said thus, he gave up the ghost.

47Now when the centurion saw what was done, he glorified God, saying, Certainly this was a righteous man. 48And all the people that came together to that sight, beholding the things which were done, smote their breasts, and returned. 49And all his acquaintance, and the women that followed him from Galilee, stood afar off, beholding these things.

50And, behold, *there was* a man named Joseph, a counsellor; *and he was* a good man, and a just: 51(the same had not consented to the counsel and deed of them;) *he was* of Arimathaea, a city of the Jews: who also himself waited for the kingdom of God. 52This *man* went unto Pilate, and begged the body of Jesus. 53And he took it down, and wrapped it in linen, and laid it in a sepulchre that was hewn in stone, wherein never man before was laid. 54And that day was the preparation, and the sabbath drew on.

⁵⁵And the women also, which came with him from Galilee, followed after, and beheld the sepulchre, and how his body was laid. ⁵⁶And they returned, and prepared spices and ointments; and rested the sabbath day according to the commandment.

The resurrection and ascension of Christ

Matthew 28; Mark 16; John 20 and 21

24 Now upon the first *day* of the week, very early in the morning, they came unto the sepulchre, bringing the spices which they had prepared, and certain *others* with them. ²And they found the stone rolled away from the sepulchre. ³And they entered in, and found not the body of the Lord Jesus. ⁴And it came to pass, as they were much perplexed thereabout, behold, two men stood by them in shining garments: ⁵and as they were afraid, and bowed down *their* faces to the earth, they said unto them, Why seek ye the living among the dead? ⁶He is not here, but is risen: remember how he spake unto you when he was yet in Galilee, ⁷saying, The Son of man must be delivered into the hands of sinful men, and be crucified, and the third day rise again.

⁸And they remembered his words, ⁹and returned from the sepulchre, and told all these things unto the eleven, and to all the rest. ¹⁰It was Mary Magdalene, and Joanna, and Mary *the mother* of James, and other *women that were* with them, which told these things unto the apostles. ¹¹And their words seemed to them as idle tales, and they believed them not.

¹²Then arose Peter, and ran unto the sepulchre; and stooping down, he beheld the linen clothes laid by themselves, and departed, wondering in himself at that which was come to pass.

¹³And, behold, two of them went that same day to a village called Emmaus, which was from Jerusalem *about* threescore furlongs. ¹⁴And they talked together of all these things which had happened. ¹⁵And it came to pass, that, while they communed *together* and reasoned, Jesus himself drew near, and went with them. ¹⁶But their eyes were holden that they should not know him. ¹⁷And he said unto them, What manner of communications *are* these that ye have one to another, as ye walk, and are sad?

¹⁸And the one of them, whose name was Cleopas, answering

said unto him, Art thou only a stranger in Jerusalem, and hast not known the things which are come to pass there in these days? [19]And he said unto them, What things? And they said unto him, Concerning Jesus of Nazareth, which was a prophet mighty in deed and word before God and all the people: [20]and how the chief priests and our rulers delivered him to be condemned to death, and have crucified him. [21]But we trusted that it had been he which should have redeemed Israel: and beside all this, to day is the third day since these things were done. [22]Yea, and certain women also of our company made us astonished, which were early at the sepulchre; [23]and when they found not his body, they came, saying, that they had also seen a vision of angels, which said that he was alive. [24]And certain of them which were with us went to the sepulchre, and found *it* even so as the women had said: but him they saw not.

[25]Then he said unto them, O fools, and slow of heart to believe all that the prophets have spoken: [26]ought not Christ to have suffered these things, and to enter into his glory? [27]And beginning at Moses and all the prophets, he expounded unto them in all the scriptures the things concerning himself.

[28]And they drew nigh unto the village, whither they went: and he made as though he would have gone further. [29]But they constrained him, saying, Abide with us: for it is toward evening, and the day is far spent. And he went in to tarry with them. [30]And it came to pass, as he sat at meat with them, he took bread, and blessed *it*, and brake, and gave to them. [31]And their eyes were opened, and they knew him; and he vanished out of their sight. [32]And they said one to another, Did not our heart burn within us, while he talked with us by the way, and while he opened to us the scriptures?

[33]And they rose up the same hour, and returned to Jerusalem, and found the eleven gathered together, and them that were with them, [34]saying, The Lord is risen indeed, and hath appeared to Simon. [35]And they told what things *were done* in the way, and how he was known of them in breaking of bread.

[36]And as they thus spake, Jesus himself stood in the midst of them, and saith unto them, Peace *be* unto you. [37]But they were terrified and affrighted, and

supposed that they had seen a spirit. [38]And he said unto them, Why are ye troubled? and why do thoughts arise in your hearts? [39]Behold my hands and my feet, that it is I myself: handle me, and see; for a spirit hath not flesh and bones, as ye see me have. [40]And when he had thus spoken, he shewed them *his* hands and *his* feet.

[41]And while they yet believed not for joy, and wondered, he said unto them, Have ye here any meat? [42]And they gave him a piece of a broiled fish, and of an honeycomb. [43]And he took *it*, and did eat before them.

[44]And he said unto them, These *are* the words which I spake unto you, while I was yet with you, that all things must be fulfilled, which were written in the law of Moses, and *in* the prophets, and *in* the psalms, concerning me. [45]Then opened he their understanding, that they might understand the scriptures, [46]and said unto them, Thus it is written, and thus it behoved Christ to suffer, and to rise from the dead the third day: [47]and that repentance and remission of sins should be preached in his name among all nations, beginning at Jerusalem. [48]And ye are witnesses of these things. [49]And, behold, I send the promise of my Father upon you: but tarry ye in the city of Jerusalem, until ye be endued with power from on high.

[50]And he led them out as far as to Bethany, and he lifted up his hands, and blessed them. [51]And it came to pass, while he blessed them, he was parted from them, and carried up into heaven. [52]And they worshipped him, and returned to Jerusalem with great joy: [53]and were continually in the temple, praising and blessing God. Amen.